BRITAIN IN PICTURES
A History and Bibliography

For Sheila Shannon

Britain in Pictures
A HISTORY AND BIBLIOGRAPHY

MICHAEL CARNEY

LONDON
WERNER SHAW LTD
1995

Colour photographs for the four colour plates were supplied by
Bromhead Photography, Bristol.

© Michael Carney, 1995
ISBN 0 907961 09 6

Printed and bound in Great Britain for
the publishers, Werner Shaw Ltd,
26 Charing Cross Road (Suite 34),
London WC2H 0DH by
St Edmundsbury Press, Bury St Edmunds, Suffolk

Typeset in 10 on 12 pt Janson by Alacrity Phototypesetters,
Banwell Castle, Weston-super-Mare, Avon.

Contents

Introduction and Acknowledgements 7

PART 1 THE HISTORY
    Modest Delights 13
    Whose Idea? 16
    The Best Sort of Propaganda 28
    Getting Started 30
    Keeping Going 33
    Walter Turner's Contribution 39
    A Magnificent Achievement:
        Subjects 41
        1939-45 War 43
        Illustrations 45
        Authors and their Writing 50
        Critics' Reception 57

    What Sort of Britain — Or England? 57

PART 2 THE BOOKS
    Introduction 65
    Details Common to all the Books 66
    Conventions Used in Chronological List 70
    Chronological List of Books and Authors 75
    Sales Figures 120
    List of Authors and Editors 124
    Subject List 128

INDEX 133

ILLUSTRATIONS
    Hilda Matheson 12
    Wolfgang Foges, Walter Neurath and Adprint meeting 24
    W.J. Turner and Sheila Shannon 40
    W.J. Turner 64
    The Seven Omnibus Volumes *facing page* 32
    The Six English Poets and other rare editions *facing page* 33
    Some of the British People Volumes *facing page* 64
    The Seven Commonwealth Volumes *facing page* 65

Introduction and Acknowledgements

Part 1 consists of a short essay which records the history of 'Britain In Pictures' (BIP) and provides an assessment. Part 2 comprises a bibliography in three sections: first a chronological list of all the books with information about each volume, its author and sales; secondly a list of authors; and thirdly a subject list. Each list provides cross references. Finally there is an index to both parts. Numbers in round brackets after book titles in the text refer to where the title can be found in the chronological list. Other numbers refer to footnotes. It would have been satisfying to show many of the fine illustrations which appeared in all the BIP books. In addition to considerations of cost, however, there was also a severe problem of selection. To demonstrate reasonably the range and variety of nearly 4,000 British paintings, drawings, prints, manuscripts and photographs which were reproduced in the books would require a volume on its own; and a small, unrepresentative, selection would have misled readers and collectors who are not familiar with the books. So illustrations are limited to photographs of the principals and some of the books they edited, designed and produced.

I am very grateful to the people who have helped me. Collins, the publisher, destroyed sometime in the 1950s nearly all their records relating to BIP, but they were able to provide me with a list of titles and authors which was my starting point. I would like to acknowledge also help I received from individuals in the following organisations: the International Council for Canadian Studies and the National Library of Canada, the Pakistan Embassy, the India Office Library, The Walmsley Society, the University College of Wales Aberystwyth, *The Times* Library, The Scout Association, The Royal Horticultural Society, The Jockey Club and The British Library Map Library.

Government records in the Public Records Office at Kew contained information which helped in understanding how the series originated as part of Britain's war-time propaganda. I made use of Foreign Office papers FO 898 pieces 1, 3-8, 19, 41-44, 50-52; The Lord President's Committee minutes and papers and the Sub-committee on the Supply of Books, CAB 71 and 75 pieces 1-4, 28; Home Policy Committee Minutes and Papers CAB 75 pieces 1-14; and Ministry of Information INF 1 pieces 1-3, 8-10, 13, 123, 135, 169-170, 230, 358. The British Library's Newspaper Library at Colindale was also a fruitful source and I consulted there the *News Chronicle* for 1931; *The Times* 1940-41; *The Listener* 1941; the *New Statesman and Nation* 1940-41; *The Spectator* 1940-41; *The Observer* 1940-50; and *The Times Literary Supplement* 1940-50.

I have drawn on articles by Richard Dalby in *The Book and Magazine Collector* of May 1984 and October 1993 and Brian Mills in *The Antiquarian Book Monthly Review* of October 1986; and on two articles in *The Private Library*, one by Peter Eads in the autumn edition 1986, the other by D.E. Wickham in the autumn edition 1987, each of whom also provided more information when I wrote to them. John Kinnane, then editor of the re-named *Antiquarian Book Monthly*, helped in several ways; and as a result of my letters which he kindly published in that journal in June 1993 and April 1994, and of another in the *Royal Air Force Journal* of May 1994, I received information from a large number of people, unfortunately too many to list, who were especially helpful about authors who are not included in reference books; but I must thank Neil Ritchie, who wrote from South Africa at an early stage of my researches with useful guidance on sources, and Ian Jackson of California who made many worthwhile suggestions. Joseph S. F. Murdoch of Pennsylvania, USA, who also generously filled three gaps in my collection of the Commonwealth series, Paul Breman, a London bookseller who has built up several complete sets of BIP, and Michael Sedgley of Sussex, each sent me their complete lists of the editions they had collected; and Mr Breman kindly loaned me volumes to photograph. Juliet Hobbs the daughter of Randal Burdon who was Ngaio Marsh's co-author of *New Zealand* (26), Robert Ives the son of Arthur Ives who wrote *British Hospitals* (131), and Edmund Marsden the son of Christopher Marsden who wrote *The English at the Seaside* (112), provided biographical details about their fathers, and Mr Marsden loaned me the Turkish translation of *English Farming* (16) to photograph. Mrs M.S. Tangye, widow of Nigel Tangye who wrote *Britain in the Air* (68), gave me details about her husband. Mr Nigel Nicolson helped greatly by providing the photograph of Hilda Matheson and loaning papers, in particular a memorial volume about her, published by the Hogarth Press, which is not widely known.

One of the key figures responsible for the design of the books was Mr Walter Neurath who worked at the time for the producer Adprint. His wife, Mrs Eva Neurath, who worked with him on some of the books, is still living and chairs the fine art publishing company of Thames and Hudson which they founded together when he left Adprint in 1946. I am grateful to her for the help she gave me, answering my questions with infinite patience. Mrs Alice Harrap, Adprint's first employee, and Ruth Rosenberg and Joyce Howell who worked there with her, also helped considerably with memories and documents about Adprint and

Introduction and Acknowledgements 9

its founder, Wolfgang Foges, who played a significant role in getting BIP started. His son, Peter Foges now living in New York, also helped.

Of the 117 authors, I was able to locate only thirteen still living — Janet Adam Smith (Mrs J. Carleton) who wrote *Life Among the Scots* (101) and *Children's Illustrated Books* (126); Peter Bicknell, *British Hills and Mountains* (116); Charles Hadfield who, with Frank Eyre, now dead, wrote *English Rivers and Canals* (84); Jacquetta Hawkes (Mrs J.B. Priestley), *Early Britain* (92); John Hislop, *The Turf* (129) (Mr Hislop died in February 1994 shortly after I spoke to him); John Herbert, *The Port of London* (115); Derek Hudson, *British Journalists and Newspapers* (86); Elspeth Huxley, *East Africa* (6); Margaret Lambert and Enid Marx, who jointly wrote *English Popular and Traditional Art* (102); R.M. Lockley, *Islands Around Britain* (85); John Russell, *British Portrait Painters* (76); and Dame Veronica Wedgwood, *Battlefields in Britain* (78). I am grateful to those authors who helped me. In particular, Mr Hadfield had kept correspondence from 1944-45 relating to his book and when I met him I was able to obtain information from these papers as well as from his memory. There are four authors about whom I have been unable to find any biographical details; it is possible that some of these too are still living and, if so, I apologise to them for my omissions.

Anne Scott-James (Lady Lancaster), whose proposed BIP book on textiles was never finished because its completion was pre-empted by the ending of the series, was the first person to guide me to Sheila Shannon, officially the Secretary to 'Britain In Pictures', though in fact the Assistant General Editor to Walter Turner after Hilda Matheson's death. Now Mrs Dickinson, widow of the poet and broadcaster Patric Dickinson, and living in Rye, Sheila Shannon agreed to meet me in the summer of 1993, having previously considered a number of questions I sent to her about the history of the project. The other principals who were involved being dead, none of the records having been kept by the publisher, other sources such as correspondence, Government records, newspaper articles and book reviews of the time being rather meagre, the only significant, detailed source of information about BIP other than the books themselves and the other, few, survivors, is Sheila Shannon's memory. Her central role in the project has been verified by the surviving authors who well remember Sheila's assistance during the publication of their own volume and urged me to contact her. R.M. Lockley (already referred to) wrote from New Zealand where he is now living, and still writing, and said that it was 'an easy book' because of all the help he received. Sheila Shannon was 79 years of age when I met her and was still as vigorous and alert as I imagine her to have been between 1940 and 1947 when she co-ordinated the General Editor, the publisher, the producer and all the authors to such good effect. I owe her an immense debt of gratitude for giving me the benefit of her memories during our discussions and for her suggestions on my text.

Despite all this help, gaps remain. There is no further systematic way now of filling them; additional information will come, if at all, by happy accident. In the circumstances it seemed better to publish, allowing readers to provide more information and correct mistakes. Needless to say, any mistakes are entirely my own and not the fault of people who helped me.

Michael Carney
Bristol, January 1995

PART 1 THE HISTORY

Hilda Matheson
(*photograph by Howard Coster reproduced by courtesy of Mr Nigel Nicolson*)

MODEST DELIGHTS

In May 1940, when the war seemed to be as phoney as ever, the Sadler's Wells Ballet set out to tour Holland and the Western Front. On their first night in The Hague, the dancers were showered with flowers; on their second night, at Hengelo near the German border, they were spat upon and jeered in the streets. On the morning of 10 May after their return to The Hague they woke up to the roar of planes and gunfire; and from the roof of their hotel watched German parachutists drop in the light of a burning Rotterdam. There followed a nightmare drive to a port near Amsterdam when, gratuitously adding to the actual horrors all round, Robert Helpman announced that he had just seen a new moon through glass. All the Company got back to Britain on a cargo boat, but it had been a near thing as the real war started in earnest.[1] Throughout that spring, autumn and winter the survival of Britain and the British way of life was challenged as never before. Hitler seemed to be intent not just on destroying the nation and its historic buildings, but also obliterating any record of its very existence. On 29 December 1940, between five and six million books were estimated to have been destroyed in a single bombing raid on London, some three to four million in Stationers' Hall alone.[2] Hitler was winning also another war of words as Joseph E. Kennedy, the American Ambassador to Britain, reported to Washington that Britain was finished, and left his London post for good in October 1940.[3]

Whilst the Sadler's Wells Company had been arranging its ill-timed visit to the front-line, the Planning and Broadcasting Committee of the Government's new Ministry of Information was meeting to consider the sort of propaganda likely to be needed to put Britain's case to the world. Mr. Dunkerley, one of the senior civil servants involved:

> ... said that the BBC had heard of some talking birds who could be trained to imitate German Leaders. Mr. Ingrams ... mentioned a gramophone record of a jungle war dance in which the voice of the medicine man was identical to that of Goebbels. Mr. Dunkerley agreed to find out whether any of these ideas had been followed up.[4]

---

[1] Account by Miss Amabel Farjeon of the corps de ballet quoted in *The English Ballet* (80), pp 12-14.
[2] Described by Stanley Unwin in *The Spectator* January 1941.
[3] *Keesing's Contemporary Archives* Vol 1940-41, p 4462.
[4] Planning and Broadcasting minutes March 1940.

In another part of the same Ministry, a woman named Hilda Matheson was considering the same problem of propaganda, and coming to the conclusion that something rather more effective than talking birds was required. The result of her thinking was one of the great publishing achievements of any age, 'Britain In Pictures' (BIP).

BIP is the collective title for three series of illustrated books launched in March 1941, the individual series being 'The British People In Pictures' (BP), 'The British Commonwealth In Pictures' (BC), and 'The English Poets In Pictures' (EP). By 1950, the year in which the last volume was issued, six titles in the Poets, seven in the Commonwealth and 113 in the People series had been published, a total of 126 books, most of which were published during the war. In addition to the individual volumes, there was an omnibus volume containing all the Commonwealth series and six other omnibus volumes each containing either six or seven volumes from the People series. Nearly three million copies were sold, many of them overseas particularly in the United States of America, in countries of the British Commonwealth and Empire and in Latin America. Some volumes were translated into other languages and copies in Spanish, Italian, French and Turkish have been seen, although it has been claimed that eleven languages were used[1]. Each book, illustrated with colour and black-and-white reproductions of British paintings, drawings, manuscripts, prints and photographs, described an important aspect of British life in such significant areas as literature, art and craftsmanship, history, education and religion, science, medicine and engineering, social life and character, country life and sport, and topographical and natural history. The authors, of whom there were 117, were either eminent novelists, poets or journalists, or authorities on a subject who could also write well. The distinctive characteristic of the series was to provide a comprehensive view in words and pictures of British life, in all its aspects, at a time when the survival of Britain as an independent nation was being threatened. Each volume, within a limit of only 48 pages, was authoritative, superbly written and beautifully illustrated. The books were also very cheap, those in the Poets series selling initially for 2s 6d (12½p) each and in the other two series for 3s 6d (17½p) each. The result was a library of superb, illustrated essays about Britain which still instructs and pleases today.

The success of BIP at the time, and the enduring value of the books since, is perhaps due more to the words than to the pictures. The pictures are a delight, but it is in the essays which accompany them that the British character and its

---

[1] Brian Mills, 'Some Notes on the Story of Adprint', *Antiquarian Book Monthly Review*, October 1986.

The History 15

achievements come to life. Despite the title of the series, the pictures by themselves would do scant justice to the riches of Britain and its peoples, although they are an important and very attractive supplement to the text. In fact, the series demonstrates that Britain is best represented through its common language, the English language. According to Lord David Cecil, English '... is a poet's language ... ideally suited for description ...'[1] This capacity of the language is used to good effect in the essays which form the core of each book.

Some of the writers who contributed are unduly modest about their 'little book'. For example, the distinguished historians Dame Veronica Wedgwood and G. M. Young, as well as one or two others, did not include the BIP volume when listing their publications for *Who's Who*. When I wrote to Dame Veronica in June 1993, her companion replied with some helpful information, but added that her book on *Battlefields in Britain* (78) was of course 'small beer' and 'a rather unimportant part of her oeuvre'. Many historians would be pleased to offer Dame Veronica's small beer as their finest claret; her essay, like so many in the series, is superb. It is a model of historical writing, displaying that sense of the past and imaginative mind that she insists at the start of the essay are so necessary to successful history. She assesses the impact on battles of natural features such as mountains, rivers and ravines, the influence of man-made objects such as houses, castles and weapons, and the effect above all of individual people: 'We are concerned only with recapturing men in action and the landscape of their time'. Of action there is plenty. Her descriptions of the major land-based battles in Britain from Hastings in 1066 to Culloden in 1746 are full of martial excitement, shrewd strategic assessments, and vivid pen-portraits of fighting men and their leaders. The account of Montrose's winter march in 1645 down Glen Roy and over the foothills of Ben Nevis to surprise and overcome Argyll's much bigger army at Inverlochy must be one of the finest descriptions of what John Buchan called 'one of the great exploits in the history of British arms'. Dame Veronica possesses, as *The Times Literary Supplement* reviewer wrote in February 1945, '... an instinct for the realities of war denied to many historians of the belligerent sex'. Today's history students would do well to read her book and marvel at the quality of writing which, in only 48 pages, some of them taken up with illustrations, describes a monumental subject so clearly and elegantly, with space even to comment on the often decisive influence of the British weather:

> ... fog at Barnet, a March snowstorm at Towton, a blustering wet August for King Charles's Cornish campaign in 1664, the soft Highland mists which blotted out

---

[1] *The English Poets* (1), p 7 (not part of the Poets series).

Culloden and swathed Auldearn; the 'deluge of dropping showers' at Dunbar; the occasional dazzling summer day — Naseby fought on June 14th 1645, Killiecrankie on July 27th 1689.

Dame Veronica's modesty about her 'little book' is matched by the unassuming, but striking, appearance of the books themselves, and by the clear, simple, almost diffident, way in which large themes are tackled without pomposity. Inside these slim volumes, with their well-designed jackets, covers, type and illustrations, it is often the small, unassertive aspects of British life which most delight the authors. Ronald Lockley, writing about *Islands Round Britain* (85), says his book is intended '... to describe some of the more interesting small islands which are as yet little known, but which catch the imagination with their suggestion of remote charm.' Whilst describing the Thames, the Severn and the Trent as well as the great canals between the great cities, Frank Eyre and Charles Hadfield in their book *English Rivers and Canals* (84) are captivated most by the smaller rivers which '... like England itself ... have had an influence upon the world's history out of all proportion to their size.' They go on to say that 'We in this Island have always had an especial affection for the little things of life...'. That affection shines through most of the books. In her description of *Early Britain* (92), when there was scarcely a metropolis of any size, it is 'the tribal capitals', the 'generally humbler towns', that Jacquetta Hawkes finds most interesting. This gravitation towards the small, the local, the particular, is characteristic of the series, even in those volumes when the subjects being discussed are on an heroic scale. The display of such typical British reserve and modesty seems very appropriate in books published to describe Britain and its achievements. Those achievements were often glorious, but the authors refrain from glorying in them.

Also characteristic of the series is good English prose. In this respect, Dame Veronica's excellent essay is not unique; and it would not be excessive to say that the series provides some of the best essays in the language.

WHOSE IDEA?

The originator of the idea for a series of short, illustrated books about Britain was Hilda Matheson, at the time engaged on propaganda work for the new Ministry of Information. She was one of three people who formed the first editorial committee of BIP; the other two were Walter Turner (W.J. Turner), poet, writer and journalist, who later acted as the General Editor, and Dorothy Wellesley, poet and writer, who was shortly to become Duchess of Wellington.

The History 17

They had an advisory committee of four members; Lord David Cecil, a distinguished academic and literary critic who also contributed one volume to the series (1), but as an adviser was a 'sleeping partner', rarely attending meetings or answering letters[1]; Sir Ronald Storrs, the diplomat and arabist, much referred to by T.E. Lawrence in *Seven Pillars of Wisdom*, who was said to be very sociable '... with quick, almost feminine perceptions'[2]; and Sir Frederick Whyte, who in 1939 had become Head of the American Division of the Ministry of Information after a rather unusual career which had included four years as Political Adviser to the National Government of China[3]. The author, Sir Hugh Walpole, also advised for a brief period until his death in 1941[4]. The Secretary to Hilda Matheson was Sheila Shannon, who later acted as Assistant General Editor. The first ten volumes were 'Published for Penns In The Rocks Press by William Collins Of London' and the subsequent volumes simply by 'William Collins of London' (sometimes with minor variations on that imprint, for details of which see Part 2). All the books were produced by Adprint Limited London, founded in 1937 by Wolfgang Foges. These are the basic facts. Sorting out the various relationships and responsibilities is not easy, given the paucity of records about the series, and what follows includes some supposition.

Hilda Matheson was born on 7 June 1888, a clergyman's daughter who later read History at Oxford as a member not of a college, but of the Society of Oxford Home-Students. This was '... in the quiet days before the Great War when women were not yet full members of the University'.[5] By 1939, when she began to develop her ideas for a propaganda series, she had had experience of intelligence operations during the 1914-18 war, became immersed in political life and public administration, and gained extensive experience of producing short, pithy, accounts of important subjects in her role as Director of Talks for the BBC.

Sheila Shannon described her as a woman who was 'always in over-drive'. In July 1914 she had given up her job of 'secretary to Mr Hogarth at the

---

[1] Sheila Shannon's phrase.
[2] Sir Ronald Henry Amherst Storrs KCMG, b 14 November 1881, d 1 November 1955, ed Charterhouse School and Pembroke College Oxford. Egyptian civil service then Governor of Jerusalem (1917), Cyprus (1926) and Northern Rhodesia (1932).
[3] Sir Alexander Frederick Whyte, b 30 September 1883, d 30 July 1970. Liberal MP for Perth city 1910-1918. Later worked in India and China before becoming Director-General of The English Speaking Union in 1938.
[4] Sir Hugh Seymour Walpole, b 13 March 1884, d 1 June 1941, novelist. His brief membership of the advisory committee, unlike the others, is not recorded on BIP notepaper, but is listed in an Adprint/Collins contract of 1941 shown me by Peter Eads.
[5] *Hilda Matheson* pub Hogarth Press 1941, pp 9-14 and 15-16.

Ashmolean Museum in Oxford' in order to serve in the war, first in a military hospital, and later in the War Office where she carried out special intelligence work for MI5. One of her tasks was to set up in Rome a proper office on the lines of MI5 in London. 'The Italian authorities were very incredulous about the capacity of a young girl, for she did look most absurdly young then, to do such work.' Public life, including its battles and intrigues, obviously proved congenial, because although she refused to continue with MI5 after the war, she was persuaded to become political secretary to Lady Astor, Britain's first woman MP, or at least the first to take her seat in the House. For Lady Astor '... those first years in Parliament were only made possible by (Hilda Matheson's) unremitting work and service, not for me, but for the cause of women ... she was really completely magnificent and we worked as one'. This work extended Hilda Matheson's already wide circle of friends and acquaintances which later proved invaluable for BIP. People who knew her always commented on the fact that she 'knew everybody'. Her mother recalled Hilda's excitement after 'meeting Lawrence, back the day before from the taking of Damascus' and who had just spent the morning with the King and Lloyd George telling them all about it.[1]

Harold Nicolson in his Diaries recalled 'a damp walk' with Hilda just before dinner; he records that '... Tom Mosley was present and announced that he will shortly launch his manifesto practically creating the National Party.' She was one of the three most frequent visitors to Harold Nicolson's wife, Victoria Sackville-West, at their homes Long Barn and Sissinghurst, the other two being Virginia Woolf and Dorothy Wellesley. He refers often in his diaries to Hilda Matheson and in one entry ruminates about the possibility of his writing a novel of diplomacy and character in which there would be a Secretary of State, unctuous, evangelical and insecure, who would be modelled on Joynson Hicks, and 'a woman under-secretary of the type of Hilda Matheson.'[2]

This high regard for her abilities was generally shared and, because of it, Lady Astor and other friends persuaded her to accept (Lord) Reith's pressing invitations to join the BBC. They thought that she would be an effective pioneer of radio communication, and they were right. She was the first Director of Talks from January 1927 to October 1931. Vernon Bartlett MP described admiringly how she '... acquired great experience in the art of expressing rather unorthodox views in words that would not shock orthodox minds ... In the Savoy Hill days we were pioneers. Every few months the engineers would produce a new

[1] *Hilda Matheson* op cit pp 9-14 and 15-16.
[2] *Harold Nicolson's Diaries and Letters 1930-39*, edit Nigel Nicolson, pub Collins 1966, pp 49, 61, and 117.

The History

type of microphone; Hilda Matheson would produce a new kind of talk ... she would argue and wheedle until the authorities, reluctant to spend money on developments they did not altogether like, were prepared to allow us to try another talk from abroad'.[1] In his *History of Broadcasting in the United Kingdom*, Asa Briggs refers to her '... leaving a very powerful imprint on the BBC.'[2] She was described by the *News Chronicle* as one of the cleverest as well as the best dressed women in the BBC, '... seldom seen in her office without her pet dog — a spaniel'.[3] Liberal-minded, brilliantly intelligent, energetic, and with her vast range of interesting and influential contacts, she introduced to the programme of BBC talks some of the country's best speakers and writers. The *New Statesman* in a later appreciation described her as '... the remarkable woman who built up the intellectual reputation of the BBC in the days when it was still at Savoy Hill ... she 'knew everyone' at a time when Sir John Reith, whose first job was organisation, was still out of touch with the literary and educational world. She collected a brilliant staff; she brought to the microphone all the leaders of British thought. She was not always tactful.'[4] The lack of tact was to be her undoing at the BBC. At first, the relationship with (Lord) Reith went well, and on one occasion, after hearing him make a major speech, she told him that one day he would surely be Prime Minister.[5] Her dynamic and intelligent approach to the new medium of radio made her a very valuable member of his staff. She was genuinely interested in ideas as well as people and she saw that 'Talks' offered a special opportunity. Her ideas on how radio should be used are set out in her book 'Broadcasting' published in 1933 after her work with the BBC ended in rancour and recrimination.

Those ideas, and also her resignation, are relevant to her later work on BIP because of the light they throw on her analytical approach to communication as well as on her character and temperament. She welcomed speakers of every kind and helped them to express themselves in the new medium, the nature of which she analysed carefully. In her book she said that most speakers needed a script if they were to avoid tiresome verbosity, repetition and hesitation. 'A technique had to be found which would avoid the pitfalls of impromptu speech and yet retain its atmosphere.' It was especially important to prepare a talk and not a treatise or essay so that the script sounded as though it was spoken to a person and not to a public meeting.[6] No doubt she applied the same thoughtful and

---

[1] *Hilda Matheson* op cit pp 22-26.
[2] Vol 2 *The Golden Age of Wireless* pp 124-7, pub OUP 1965.
[3] *News Chronicle* 3 December 1931. The dog's name was Torquil.
[4] *New Statesman and Nation* 16 November 1940.
[5] *The Expense of Glory: A Life of John Reith* by Ian McIntyre pub Harper-Collins 1993.
[6] *Broadcasting* by Hilda Matheson, pp 76-77, pub Thornton Butterworth in HUL series 1933.

analytical approach to the nature of propaganda and to how a series of short, illustrated books could best be designed for their intended audience.

When she resigned from the BBC some commentators suggested that she was obliged to leave because of political hostility towards BBC talks which were, then as now, often accused of left-wing bias. The *News Chronicle* explained her resignation as a '... struggle of a woman against a management of men ... Miss Matheson has pressed her views from a feminine standpoint in the face of overwhelming masculine opposition'.[1] One of her staff at the time, Lionel Fielden, who owed to her his appointment to the BBC after he botched his interview with (Lord) Reith, recorded his recollection of the resignation in a book he published in 1960 as follows: (Lord) Reith '... sent sharp little notes to Hilda suggesting that so-and-so held eccentric or subversive or atheistic or anarchistic views and was not a suitable person for the microphone. Hilda, jealous of her friends, retorted no less sharply, and the battle was on. Reith soon reached the point of saying that so-and-so was not to broadcast. Hilda replied that he didn't have enough culture to know what he was talking about. I became a highly uncomfortable buffer state, trying at one moment to persuade Reith that Hilda was valuable to the BBC, and at another trying to stop Hilda from writing offensive memoranda. It was all to no purpose: Hilda was forced into resignation, and left the BBC for ever.'[2] According to Asa Briggs it was mainly a matter of personalities. As she lost her monopoly of the spoken word following reorganisations, there was a good deal of bad temper and jealousy. She proved testy and difficult to cooperate with and recriminations multiplied on all sides. When she submitted her resignation on 12 October 1931, (the official announcement was delayed until December), the Director General, (Lord) Reith '... was very glad indeed to see her go'.[3]

She later joined the Royal Institute of International Affairs at Chatham House and worked on the *African Survey*. Due to the illness of Lord Hailey, who commented on her untiring energy '... joined to a rare capacity for rapid decision',[4] she took on the responsibility for completing the *Survey*,[5] an enormous record of nearly 2,000 pages, for which work she was awarded the OBE. However, it was the outbreak of war in 1939 and the build up of preparations beforehand which provided, for a short period at least, the greatest outlet for her vast energy and creativity and led to the publication of BIP.

[1] *News Chronicle* 3 December 1931.
[2] *The Natural Bent* by Lionel Fielden, pub Andre Deutsch, p 116.
[3] Asa Briggs op cit pp 141-143.
[4] *Hilda Matheson*, op cit pp 43-45.
[5] Letter to *The Times* 7 November 1940 from Sir Julian Huxley.

'In November 1939', as her mother remembered it,[1] 'before she was really quite clear of the *Survey*, a mysterious man began calling her up but would give no name. Finally they met. When she came back from lunching with him she told me laughingly that he was a man who seemingly knew everything she had done all her life ... Finally ... she went reluctantly into a very embryonic propaganda work connected with MI. The last work she undertook was in connection with foreign propaganda, both in the form of editing a series of books for world-wide distribution, and in directing foreign broadcasts.' With the support first of the Foreign Office, and then of the Ministry of Information, she began to organise in her ferociously energetic way the various propaganda activities that she judged were now necessary. She was the first Director of the Joint Broadcasting Committee (JBC) formed in 1939. Nominally it was set up to promote international understanding by means of broadcasting, but in fact its main task was to diffuse constructive propaganda about Britain through the broadcasting systems of other countries. Her role in this work, and the forceful way in which she pursued it, were bitterly resented by BBC staff. With her usual flair and energy she recruited foreign nationals, often emigrés from the Nazi and Fascist dictatorships, and used them to communicate material put together by her team.[2] At the same time she was developing BIP as part of her propaganda work, being concerned to provide accurate information about Britain in support of the war effort.

The books reflected her interest in ideas and the arts as well as her assessment of the propaganda needs of the time. The concept of short, attractively illustrated essays, written by the best writers and authorities available, who would be guided to present their work in a way that was appropriate to a popular series and a wide audience, was undoubtedly hers. Virginia Woolf remembered that '... she asked me to write some damned book for some damned series. It was to be patriotic; at the same time intellectual; also badly paid'.[3] It is likely that it was she who laid down the tight specification for the balance of pictures and words in each volume within a total of only 48 pages, a scheme which survived until the end of the series, although the designers at Adprint would also have influenced the format.

She was able to realise her ideas with the help of Dorothy Wellesley, wife of Lord Gerald Wellesley who, in 1943, was to succeed his nephew as Seventh Duke of Wellington. Writing in the *Dictionary of National Biography*, Victoria

---

[1] *Hilda Matheson* op cit pp 9-14.
[2] Minutes of Min. of Inf. Policy Committee, 13 February 1941.
[3] 14 November 1940, *The Letters of Virginia Woolf, 1936-1941*, Vol 6, edit Nigel Nicolson, pub The Hogarth Press 1980.

Sackville-West described Dorothy Wellesley as a natural rebel with a passionate love of beauty in all its forms. Her friend, Sir George Goldie, after examining her scalp when she was eleven years old, informed her that she had the three bumps of temper, pride and combativeness more developed than in anyone he had ever known. She was a born romantic, but the bad fairy at her christening had decreed that her intellectual power should never equal her gifts of imagination; as a result, her poems, which she dashed off as fast as she could write them down, never received the revision that they demanded. This generous, enthusiastic and fiery spirit was always ready to lend support to the artistic or intellectual plans of others, and especially to those of her dear friend, Hilda Matheson. Dorothy Wellesley delighted in entertaining her friends, first at Sherfield Court in Hampshire, later at Penns in the Rocks, her home in Withyham near Groombridge in Sussex. The name of the house came from its association with the Quaker, William Penn, who had married the heiress to the property. A farm on the estate, Rocks Farm, occupied by Hilda Matheson, sometimes provided accommodation for Sheila Shannon as well as some JBC staff.[1] Penns in the Rocks had long been a centre of artistic life under Dorothy Wellesley's passionate sponsorship. Her own poetry and other writing were sometimes published under the imprint of 'Penns in the Rocks Press' and the same imprint was used for the first ten volumes of BIP published during her time of greatest involvement with the project. There was another pictorial link between her home and the series; in the grounds of the estate she had had built a small Temple to her great friend, the poet Yeats, a drawing of which was used as the publisher's device on the title pages of almost all the books in the three series from 1941 until 1950 (see Part 2 p 67 for details of variations).

The third member of the editorial team, Walter Turner (W.J. Turner), who in 1939-40 was employed by Hilda Matheson as Musical Director of the JBC[2], was another remarkable character — poet, playwright, journalist, music and drama critic. Born in Australia in October 1889, he came of a very musical family; his father was organist at Melbourne Cathedral, his mother a pianist and music teacher, and Walter Turner, although he played no instrument, was intensely musical. He was educated at Scotch College, Melbourne, and then, for a year, at the School of Mines, an uncongenial environment. After the death of his father and brother, he left for England with his mother in 1907, at the age of 17. For some years he lived in Germany, working as a tutor, and finding in pre-war Germany a musical paradise. He also travelled in France, Austria, Italy and

---

[1] Sheila Shannon told me of its use at this time.
[2] Turner's employment is recorded in a staff list attached to JBC minutes.

The History

South Africa before settling in Britain and serving in the Great War of 1914-18. He published two volumes of poetry in 1918 and with his young wife shared a home in Tite Street, London, with Siegfried Sassoon. Part of the literary and artistic life of London in the 'twenties and 'thirties, the frequent guest of Lady Ottoline Morrell at Garsington and friend of the Sitwells and their protégé William Walton, he also became a friend of the poet Yeats, through whom he first met Dorothy Wellesley. In her autobiography she records the "... many delightful evenings with him (Yeats), Mrs Yeats, W.J. Turner and Hilda Matheson.'[1] From 1916 until 1940 Walter Turner was music critic of the *New Statesman* and from 1942 until his death in 1946 literary editor of *The Spectator*. For short periods, he was also drama critic of the *London Mercury* (1919-23) and literary editor of the *Daily Herald* (1920-23).

These three creative, but volatile, people were well served by Sheila Shannon who became involved in BIP through Hilda Matheson in 1940 when plans were already well advanced for the first volumes. Born in 1913 and educated at Henrietta Barnett school, she read English at Somerville College Oxford between 1931 and 1933 and then tried a short period as a schoolmistress. In 1938 she met Allen Lane hoping to enter publishing. He showed her a mock-up of the first Penguin Book, asked if she could operate a telephone switchboard or type, noted that she could do neither, and advised her to get some office skills, regretting that he was drastically cutting editorial staff. By the end of her short period of training in a secretarial college, the declaration of war with Germany had changed employment opportunities dramatically. Armed with not very good shorthand and some acquaintance with a typewriter, Sheila applied for a job with the JBC. Her first interview with the Senior Secretary was not a success. As she was leaving, Hilda Matheson came into the room and they began talking. Finding Sheila Shannon had read English at Somerville College and wanted to find a job in publishing, and was also a friend of Mary Fisher, daughter of H.A.L. Fisher, Warden of New College, of whom Hilda Matheson was a close friend and protégé, she asked if Sheila Shannon would be interested in helping with a new series of books that she was just starting; Sheila was. Technically she was at first employed by the Foreign Office on the staff of the JBC, but her work was to help with BIP.

At the time she started in 1940, Collins and Adprint had already been appointed publisher and producer respectively. How this came about and the arrangements entered into between them and the editorial group of Matheson, Wellesley and Turner are not entirely clear. Sheila Shannon remembers

---

[1] *Far Have I Travelled*, pub James Barrie 1952 p 167.

Walter Neurath who directed for Adprint the design of BIP books, including dust-jackets, covers, type, layout and illustrations.

Wolfgang Foges, founder and Managing Director of Adprint.

A meeting at Adprint to discuss some BIP volumes.
At the far end of the table is Walter Neurath; Eva Neurath is nearest the camera; and Sir William (Billy) Collins is centre right.

regular monthly editorial conferences when she and Walter Turner would meet with Sir William Collins, who would take the chair, and two other representatives of Collins: F.T. Smith, a kindly but somewhat humourless Glaswegian Scot who worked on the editorial side, and Sidney Goldsack who looked after business and financial aspects. The meetings were friendly and 'Billy' Collins was always open to ideas, but not always easy to convince. He and Walter Turner, however, got on together extremely well.

The design of the books was profoundly influenced by a group of talented people at Adprint. Before the war, Adprint had started by producing mainly greeting cards and similar ephemera under the direction of Wolfgang Foges. Clever, tenacious, excitable and easily upset, according to Sheila Shannon he was not always easy to work with, but easy to like. He was also ambitious and keen to involve Adprint in book production. In Austria one of his innovations had been give-away fashion magazines, published in full colour and financed by fabric manufacturers. Seeing the probability of Hitler invading Austria, he had left Vienna in 1937 for London and began there to create an interest in high quality colour printing of books aimed at a popular market. The 'King Penguin' books were his idea and Adprint produced in 1939 the first five titles, printing them in Czechoslovakia, on a sale or return basis for Allen Lane who then continued the series.[1] The 'Peacock' colour books published by Collins were his idea also, but the extension of Hitler's power from Austria to Czechoslovakia cut off the sources of colour printing that he had used in those countries. He was a man bubbling over with ideas, occasionally depressive, but determined to succeed in publishing and to extend colour printing to popular books. To this end he invited to join him another talented Jewish emigré from Vienna, Walter Neurath, who had fled to Britain in 1938. Then aged 35, Walter Neurath had had considerable experience of publishing fine books during his work with the firm of Frick Verlag in Vienna, having previously studied art and philosophy at the University of Vienna. He provided the expertise in book production and design that Wolfgang Foges lacked, enabling Adprint to take on the work of producing BIP. Hilda Matheson was already a shareholder in Adprint and she was in close touch with people fleeing from the Nazi and Fascist dictatorships, using them for her JBC broadcasts. She had met Wolfgang Foges and very likely knew Walter Neurath as well as other refugees from Vienna who made a significant contribution to BIP; for example, Elisabeth Friedlander, a designer and typographer, and Elisabeth Ullman who had hoped to study medicine in Austria, but was forced to flee, like the others, for her life. The two Elisabeths

[1] ABM op cit and a note by Wolfgang Foges prepared in 1980s.

designed the distinctive dust-jackets and paper-board covers that are such an attractive feature of the books. They were joined later by Mary Petter, and Ruth Rosenberg also a refugee, who researched the pictures and designed page layouts. The work on BIP of this highly creative team under the forceful leadership of Wolfgang Foges and the expert skills of Walter Neurath resulted in several innovations in book production, including the extended design role of the producer at a time when publishers usually did everything except write the books, and the integration of text and illustration in what became known as an 'integrated' book. All of the emigrés were familiar with the famous German series of 'Blue Books' which, with their slim formats, blue covers and bold white lettering perhaps, ironically, provided some inspiration for the design of this new, British, war-time propaganda series. Adprint also provided Sheila Shannon with a secretary, Joyce Howell, to whom fell the task of co-ordinating its sometimes volatile creative artists with the equally volatile editors and the rather more down-to-earth staff of the publisher, Collins.[1]

The relationships between the various parties are a little obscure, but the evidence indicates that Collins had rather a subsidiary role. There were two agreements between Collins and Adprint dated 6 May 1940 and 7 June 1941. Adprint granted Collins an exclusive licence to publish BIP in the English language in Britain and abroad, but this did not include the right to print, which was the subject of separate agreements between printers and Adprint who also reserved a right themselves to publish in foreign countries. Adprint undertook to supply Collins with books to a strict specification at 16 pence for 3s. 6d. volumes and 12 pence for 2s. 6d. volumes. There was a separate contract between Adprint and Walter Turner dated 15 July 1941 under which the latter, in return for royalties and fees, would provide the former with edited texts. The fourth link in this chain of responsibilities was the arrangement between the editorial team and an author. Contracts with authors were made at first by the 'Editorial Committee of Penns in the Rocks Press' and later by 'the General Editor of Britain in Pictures', namely Walter Turner. Each author gave the

[1] The account of Adprint owes much to information from Alice Harrap, its first employee, and Eva Neurath, Ruth Rosenberg and Joyce Howell. Mrs Harrap is now retired having worked at Adprint until after successive takeovers it ended up as Aldus books which ceased to operate in 1983. Walter Neurath in 1946 left Adprint to set up the publishing firm Thames and Hudson which is still chaired by his wife Eva; he died on 26 September 1967. Wolfgang Foges continued in publishing until his death on 17 March 1986. Elisabeth Ullman achieved her medical ambitions, studying at evening classes to gain medical qualifications and becoming a much loved and respected tutor at St Bartholomew's Hospital. Ruth Rosenberg still works for Thames and Hudson where she retains many of the original photographs of the paintings and drawings used in the BIP volumes. Joyce Howell is retired now, having stayed as Wolfgang Foges' secretary until his death. Mary Petter is retired.

The History

Editor(s) a sole and exclusive licence to print and publish the book in the English language throughout the world and to enter into arrangements with publishers overseas for editions in languages other than English. In return the authors received an outright sum of £50 until, in 1944, this arrangement was changed to provide pro rata payments in addition for sales above 20,000. There was a further modification in 1944 when the £50 was paid in lieu of royalties for the first 10,000 copies sold, with pro rata payments for sales above that figure. Additional royalties were also paid for books included in omnibus volumes and for any published in foreign countries. According to the contract with an author, Adprint would provide the Editor with annual statements of sales to be passed on to the author. Correspondence with authors was carried out on notepaper bearing the heading 'Britain In Pictures' and the names of the members of the advisory committee. There was no reference, however, to the legal status of BIP or to links with either Collins or Adprint. Sheila Shannon says that she never had any contract of employment and that most arrangements were informal: she started on the payroll of the JBC, but later was paid by arrangements with the Editor and ultimately, for a short period after Walter Turner's death, was paid by Adprint.[1]

These various arrangements tend to confirm the answer to the question of who really was the originator of BIP. Several people have taken credit at some time for its creation. Collins always seem to have regarded it as 'theirs'; in their authorised history[2] the series is recorded as one of their great achievements. Their role as publisher was important, but limited, their greatest contributions being to ensure a regular supply of paper from their quota at a time when paper for all publications was rationed, and advising on the commercial prospects for particular volumes. Wolfgang Foges also used to claim the series as his idea, and there is sufficient evidence to support at least a claim to a very significant contribution to its development. Ruth Rosenberg thought that a polish refugee, whose name she cannot remember and who subsequently left for the USA, gave the idea to Walter Turner during a pub conversation. In fact there can be no doubt that BIP started as a propaganda idea of Hilda Matheson supported by Walter Turner and Dorothy Wellesley. It was they who developed the concept and made contractual arrangements with authors; and it was Hilda Matheson's

---

[1] Peter Eads sent me the 1941 contract between Adprint and Collins and a contract of 8 June 1948 between Adprint and Walter Turner's widow which quoted from the original contract with Turner. Nigel Nicolson sent me a photo-copy of the contract with Victoria Sackville-West (15) dated 1 January 1941; and Charles Hadfield (84) showed me his contract dated 10 May 1944 and related correspondence. According to Sheila Shannon contractual terms were the same for all authors, both eminent and less well known.
[2] *The House of Collins* by David Keir pub by Collins in 1952.

JBC budget which got it started. Being fairly free to draw on JBC monies for propaganda projects, Hilda Matheson would have been able to commission writers, to employ editorial and secretarial staff and also to enter into agreements with a publisher and producer. The JBC minutes and other papers record the occasional anguish of civil servants who never knew quite what were those 'secret' operations on which the money was spent. Her JBC budget, for a time at least, paid Sheila Shannon's salary as well as Walter Turner's. At the same time as she was developing her ideas, Wolfgang Foges was looking round for a popular series of books on which he could lavish his passion for high quality colour printing, and Walter Neurath arrived with the necessary skills. This was a fortunate conjunction of formidable, gifted personalities, supported by teams of intelligent and skilful people. By the time the first volumes were ready, Walter Turner and Sheila Shannon were to become the prime movers. However, the original driving force and the originator of the basic concept of the books — authoritative but popular, comprehensive but short, beautiful to look at but cheap — was Hilda Matheson.

THE BEST SORT OF PROPAGANDA

Behind it all, driving the project forward, was the urgent need for some systematic propaganda at the beginning of the war. Hilda Matheson, through her direction of the JBC, would have been involved in the intense debates at the time in Government circles about the sort of propaganda that was needed. There were particular anxieties in the Ministry of Information about the negative way in which the British Empire and Commonwealth was often perceived abroad. In February 1940, that Ministry was considering a report on plans for positive publicity about the Empire, including the possibility of publishing a popular pictorial book on the subject on the lines of Odham's *Story of the British People in Pictures*. The report, which was made just over a year before the launch of BIP, records that '... a number of other books on Empire subjects are impending and have been discussed by representatives of the Ministry either with the authors or with the publishers. No direct financial subvention is expected in any of these cases, but allowance must be made for expenditure on the purchase of copies of the books or pamphlets for distribution at home or abroad.' There is no evidence of any direct contractual relationship between Government and the editors, publisher and producer in order to initiate and promote the BIP series as such, but as indicated above there is plenty of evidence of substantial, indirect support. Three of the four members of the Advisory Committee had close links with the Foreign Office: Sir Frederick Whyte was, in 1939-40, Head of the American

The History

Division of the Ministry of Information; Sir Ronald Storrs had been Governor of several countries within the Empire; and even the novelist Sir Hugh Walpole had Foreign Office links from earlier years having been in charge of the Anglo-Russian propaganda bureau in Petrograd. Sir Robert Fraser, who headed the department of books in the Ministry of Information, and his assistant Max Parrish, negotiated foreign editions of BIP.[1] The overtly propagandist objectives were set out on the reverse of the dust-jackets of the first volumes as follows:

> The English have never been good at describing themselves or their ways, either for their own benefit or for the benefit of others. It is, therefore, not surprising that no comprehensive series of books, at a popular price, illustrating, in print and picture, the life, art, institutions and achievements of the British People has ever been issued, either for British or for foreign readers. At this time, when it has become essential for citizens throughout the Empire to take stock of themselves and their ideas and to express them to others, it is desirable to fill this gap.
>
> The books in these three series will be of permanent interest and, in spite of the small cost, should appeal to the book collector for the excellence of their production. It is hoped that they will contribute to the better understanding of Great Britain and the British Commonwealth.

From the start the intended audience was chiefly people abroad, especially in those countries such as the United States of America and Latin America whose citizens needed to be convinced that Britain was worth saving. The loyalty of people in the Empire and Commonwealth also had to be courted, so those countries were prime markets too. The home front was regarded as secondary, because people in Britain were assumed already to know and feel that the British way of life was worth fighting for.[2] Adprint set up an office in Nassau as a base from which to sell BIP books in the USA. One idea of Wolfgang Foges was to display them on specially constructed racks located next to news-stands in New York. The racks were to be made of wood salvaged from bombed London churches. Alice Harrap, who was well used to Foges' impetuosity ever since he asked her to postpone her wedding day so that they could have a business meeting to suit his diary, remembers many scavenging excursions before this latest idea, like the earlier meeting, was dropped. However, the Nassau office went ahead and sales to the USA developed, along with other ventures such as the production by Adprint of some special editions of the books published by BIP Bahamas (see Part 2 p 73).

One of *The Listener*'s reviewers on 20 March 1941 when the series was being

[1] ABM article and Foges' note op cit.
[2] Information on target audiences was given by Sheila Shannon.

launched commented that 'In these little books the propaganda is of the oblique and detached kind which so often succeeds where barefaced trumpet-blowing fails. Britain's best "case", after all, is her culture, her character and her democratic institutions and it is upon these elements of our national life that this new series concentrates.' Although propagandist in intention, individual volumes were never 'propaganda' in the sense of tendentious writing or an organised programme to present highly selective information. The aim was to present Britain in as many aspects as possible through the eyes of individual writers who would be free to interpret their subject, constrained only by the limitation on space and the need for ample pictorial illustrations. Nevertheless, the basic propaganda purpose was always clear and whilst authors were not directed as to tone or content, some of them obviously felt under some pressure in this respect. Ngaio Marsh,[1] writing to her co-author Randal Burdon on 28 November 1940 said 'Like you I am greatly worried by the feeling that one must introduce propaganda. We shall know more about this and get a better idea of just how much ballast of this sort is needed when we see Haskell's galley proofs of the Australian volume (5)... I should like to treat my part of the job to a fair pinch (of) irony but have no idea whether that is out of the question or not. My own feeling is that the average New Zealander (fighting forces apart) is maddeningly complacent about the war but I suppose we don't say as much to the allies and neutrals. It *is* tricky, isn't it.' She goes on to say later in the same letter 'One supposes that the freedom of the countries within the commonwealth to order their own affairs should be stressed and perhaps you could point it a little more, in your section. I think the paragraph beginning "With democracy on trial" hits the note that they want ...'

GETTING STARTED

BIP was launched in March 1941.[2] The start of such a project would have been a considerable achievement at any time, but during the blitz it must have been a desperate venture indeed. On 29 December 1940, the second great burning of the books had taken place, this time not in Germany but in the City of London. *The Observer* newspaper of 23 March 1941 reporting on the inaugural luncheon,[3] pointed out that it was being held '... not three months after that bad

---

[1] Correspondence between Ngaio Marsh and Randal Burdon copied to me by his daughter Juliet Hobbs.
[2] Eight volumes were published in March 1941; *The English Poets* (1), *British Sport* (2), *English Music* (3), *The Government Of Britain* (4), *Australia* (5), *East Africa* (6), *Shelley* (7) and *Byron* (8).
[3] The inaugural luncheon was reported by *The Spectator* on 14 March, *The Listener* on 20 March and *The Observer* on 23 March.

night when Hitler's bombers lit the second fire of London and destroyed the centre of the British book world'. In the same edition of the newspaper J.L. Garvin, was writing of 'The Empire at Stake'; and readers were urged in advertisements that 'You Can Help Me Make A Gun — Mobilise For War Work', or 'Help the Bombed Hospitals Now!'. It was at this time that '... the old and famous house of Collins shakes its head, steps out of the ashes and comes forward with as timely and bold a bit of publishing as was ever planned.' When the chief editor of Collins saw the first volumes displayed in a bookshop on the deserted seafront of a battered South Coast town, he asked himself whether they were not in fact '... the bright banners on the battlements of our island fortress or, more modestly perhaps, the defiant cockades that a nation of shopkeepers might justifiably flaunt in the faces of their book-burning foes.'[1] (Sir) Alan Herbert (A.P.H. of *Punch*), speaking at the luncheon, called the project 'The Order of the British Empire, as opposed to Hitler's vaunted New Order.' *The Observer*'s reporter said that the first eight volumes '... between them manage to distil 'the glories of our blood and state and with neither vanity nor pomp to make clear to ourselves as well as the rest of the world the full and serious nobility of our heritage'. In the desperate circumstances of the time, the high sentiment, the pride and the defiance do not seem absurdly overblown. In the same month a new American Ambassador, John Winnant, arrived and declared there was 'no place I would rather be in at this time than England.'[2]

The development of the series at this terrifying time came to rest on Walter Turner because, even before the launch, the project had lost its originator. Hilda Matheson died in a nursing home on 30 October 1940 after an operation, just five months before the first books were published. Notwithstanding *The Observer*'s references to Collins' great publishing venture, the main credit belongs to her, as was made clear at the launch by Walter Turner when he '... disclosed that the whole Britain In Pictures idea originated in the fertile brain of Hilda Matheson.'[3]

Victoria Sackville-West in a *Spectator* obituary on 22 November 1940 referred to '... that unfortunate panic at the beginning of last summer (when) some of (her staff) were snatched from her and interned. To her ordinary work, already more than enough for her tired strength, she now added the struggle to get her friends and helpers released from the camps. She succeeded indeed,

---

[1] The reaction of Collins's chief editor was recorded by David Keir in *The House of Collins* already noted.
[2] *Keesing's* op cit p 4485.
[3] *The Spectator*, 14 March 1941.

but the price she paid was her own life. When the inevitable operation had to be performed she had no longer the stamina to survive it.' She went on to say that Hilda Matheson was '... not only the best of friends, but in the noblest sense a servant of the State ... selfless, loyal, sometimes too loyal; gentle, but never weak; modest, but strong in her convictions, determined, but never aggressive ...' She had been ill for some time, 'she knew that she ought to give in, but it was not in her nature to give in. So she carried on with her job, and so she died.' Dorothy Wellesley went on to complete the editing of six volumes of 'The English Poets in Pictures', the last one being published in 1942, but played virtually no part in the rest of the series. In her autobiography she referred to her own volumes and expressed gratitude to Sheila Shannon '... who tore about the country finding unknown or scarcely known drawings, miniatures of all these poets.', but she did not refer to the other two series.[1] After Hilda Matheson's death she lost interest in the project and her name, along with Hilda Matheson's disappeared from the advertisement page of each volume, just as the imprint of Penns in the Rocks Press was discontinued from the title page. The drawing of the Temple to Yeats, the mutual friend, was retained.[2] Walter Turner was now in charge with Sheila Shannon as his assistant.

In some ways, for the success of BIP at least, this outcome was not unfortunate, although the event which occasioned it was desperately sad. The death of so creative and effective a person as Hilda Matheson at the early age of 52 was a severe blow for the country, and a very wounding loss for her friends, but it is difficult to see how Matheson, Wellesley and Turner together would have been able to sustain a project to publish more than a hundred books over a period of ten years without at some time spontaneously combusting. No one knows how BIP would have developed under the direction of this remarkable woman, but it is certain that her forceful personality would have had its way until, that is, something cracked, for it was not in her nature to manage with a light hand. Lionel Fielden recorded a different view of Hilda Matheson, referring to her running her department 'on a loose rein', but this is not borne out by other evidence, including Sheila Shannon's recollection, or, indeed, by some of Fielden's own words. There are many pictures of Hilda Matheson's complex personality which emerge from the descriptions of friends and others. To Virginia Woolf, jealous of her friendship with Victoria Sackville-West, she was '... so dried, so official', with 'Her earnest aspiring competent wooden face'.[3] A

[1] *Far Have I Travelled* op cit p 171.
[2] Except for volumes (125), (126) and (132) — see Part 2 p 67.
[3] Virginia Woolf letters op cit p 443; and diaries quoted in *Vita* by Victoria Glendinning, pub Weidenfeld and Nicolson, 1983.

The Omnibus Volumes

'The English Poets In Pictures' series and three other rare volumes, (*top to bottom*) a decorated hard cover edition of *The English Poets* (1), a Turkish translation of *British Farming* (16), and a cloth bound volume of *British Sport* (2).

very close friend of her Oxford days, Mrs H. A. L. Fisher, remembers only the 'charming creature, with her ash-gold hair and her grey eyes, her entrancing eagerness, enthusiasm and keen intelligence, her wide interests and her warm heart'. Lady Astor, who was also an admirer and remembered her huge contribution to the BBC, acknowledged other facets of her character; 'I can see her now, exhausted and white in those battles, but as firm as a rock in what she thought was right'. Sharing sometimes, perhaps, some of the qualities of the man she chose to write about in her thesis at Oxford, Savonarola. What cannot be denied is that the whole concept of BIP was hers, and without her prodigious energy and talents it would very likely never have got off the ground. Walter Turner and Sheila Shannon were now able to take it forward as she had planned it and ensure its success.[1]

KEEPING GOING

The series was envisaged as continuing for some years; when reporting its launch, *The Listener* said that the '... publishers hope that this venture will eventually provide a small library of some seventy volumes covering the whole range of our Imperial history and culture.' The editorial team usually had about ten volumes in hand at any one time as they developed the framework of subject areas (see p 41). After the first titles, most new subjects were suggested by Walter Turner. Sometimes the publisher, Collins, would draw attention at editorial meetings to subjects that ought to be included, for example, the Scout movement. Sometimes authors would suggest themselves and a particular subject. Frank Eyre and Charles Hadfield suggested one volume on rivers and canals and another on the fire services — the former was accepted, but the latter refused. Lady Cecilia Sempill suggested her book on *English Pottery and China* (77) (or *English Pottery and Porcelain*, depending on the edition). Sometimes suggestions were made by other authors in the series or by friends, thus James Fisher suggested Peter Bicknell to write *British Hills and Mountains* (116) and Derek Hudson, who wrote *British Journalists and Newspapers* (86), was suggested by a colleague of his on *The Times* who was an old friend of Walter Turner. These unsolicited offers, however, were rare. The prime originator of titles was Walter Turner and he usually proposed the authors, knowing them personally or being already an admirer of their work ... When first exploring with an author the possibility of contributing to the series, Walter Turner and Sheila Shannon would invite them to lunch at Vaiani, a Greek restaurant in

---

[1] Quotations from *Hilda Matheson* op cit, pp 39-42, 15-16.

Charlotte Street, or at the Acropolis or occasionally at the White Tower. All restaurants during the war offered a meal at the Government-controlled price of 5s.0d (25p), often a very good one. Most later meetings would take place at Yarners, a coffee shop just south of Broadcasting House. Yarners provided good coffee, Danish open sandwiches and conversation with Madame Yarner who had many devoted admirers, one of whom provided a fresh corsage of orchids each day. Despite rationing and other privations, the coffee was always plentiful and the orchids always in evidence. Here, the authors would receive what little guidance Walter Turner thought was necessary and enjoy much good conversation. Derek Hudson recalls such a luncheon '... in Charlotte Street at a place on the other side of the road to Bertorelli's' (this was Vaiani's). He remembers afterwards '... walking back with Turner to *The Spectator* office in Gower Street where he was then Literary Editor, a job in which I followed him, and I thought him and Miss Shannon very pleasant people.'[1]

Turner always took the view that having selected good writers, they should be left to get on with it with as little interference as possible. The finished manuscript was submitted to Collins by the Editor for discussion at a subsequent editorial meeting; on one occasion, Sir William Collins was rather disturbed by the way in which women were portrayed by Edith Sitwell in her volume on *English Women* (29) and asked for major revisions. The idea of requesting, much less requiring, Edith Sitwell to change her text was out of the question. When Sheila Shannon discussed this with Walter Turner later, he said that the solution was easy; he made a minor re-arrangement of some of the text to bring forward paragraphs that were, in any case, better placed at the beginning. Sir William, as expected, read only the first page or two and welcomed 'the total revision' that he had requested. All was well. Walter Turner was never daunted by such situations, rather, he relished them.[1] The main discipline on authors was not editorial interference, but the constraints imposed by a maximum of 48 pages and the need to integrate with the text appropriate illustrations. Ngaio Marsh wrote to her co-author Randall Burdon[2] '... I have pruned and pruned and can damn well prune no longer and nor can you. Now the hideous job of photographs and pictures confronts me. The floor is carpeted with atrocious glossy prints of Maori, mountain and animals.'

A year after the launch, on 29 March 1942, *The Observer* commented that '... volume has followed volume triumphantly. Brilliantly edited, expertly written, beautifully illustrated, the graceful little books really do distil the

---

[1] Discussions with Sheila Shannon and correspondence with Peter Bicknell and Derek Hudson.
[2] Marsh-Burdon correspondence op cit.

essence of our way of life, our deeds, our great heritage.' After another year, on 28 February 1943, it recorded that 'It is good to see this interesting series keep up its high standard — the 'running commentary' is lively but sound, and the illustrations are a delight.' To succeed in publishing 'volume after volume' meant overcoming year after year the impact of war. In May 1942, the War Cabinet set up a sub-committee on the supply of books because of fears that shortages of paper were making it impossible to produce worthwhile books. Publishers who were exporting books were allowed just over 37 per cent of their pre-war consumption of paper and others only 25 per cent. The Publishers' Association produced figures which showed that in 1941 the number of new books published was less than 50 per cent of the 1937 figures and the total of re-prints was less than 40 per cent.[1] The Government did not accept all the figures, but the adverse impact of the war can hardly be exaggerated. Even as late as 24 July 1944, when the end of the war was at last coming into sight, Sheila Shannon, writing tentatively to Charles Hadfield and Frank Eyre who were fire-fighters as well as authors, said that she had not liked to bother them about illustrations for their book *English Rivers and Canals* (84) '... as I have no doubt you have been more than busy since the flying bombs began.' After the war severe difficulties continued with paper rationing and general shortages of materials, but high standards continued to be maintained. Reviewing the latest volumes in *The Observer* of 15 February 1948, G.W. Stonier said that 'The balance of illustration and text, the choice of writers, the subjects covered, the production, the price: in these days such a conjunction has a touch of the miraculous.'

Sustaining this publishing marathon from 1941 to 1950 through war and the chronic shortages which followed was remarkable. A total of 133 books, including seven omnibus volumes, was published between 1941 and 1950, of which 93 were published during the war years to 1945. The number published each year, using the dates of publication shown on title pages, is set out in the table overleaf, although this is not an entirely accurate guide to publication. Despite the date given on the title page of a volume several were published in the following year. This is explained sometimes by war-time conditions with sudden shortages of essential publishing materials: '... binding is our nightmare' wrote Sheila Shannon in a letter to Charles Hadfield on 15 November 1945, 'and we have not as yet got an accurate date for publication of your book'. In the event it was published in March 1946, although the title page recorded 1945! With these reservations, the figures are:

[1] Ministry of Information papers.

Year	British People	British Commonwealth	English Poets	Omnibus Volumes	Total
1941	12	5	4	—	21
1942	17	1	2	—	20
1943	15	1	—	1	17
1944	19	—	—	—	19
1945	14	—	—	2	16
1946	12	—	—	1	13
1947	11	—	—	2	13
1948	9	—	—	1	10
1949	3	—	—	—	3
1950	1	—	—	—	1
Totals	113	7	6	7	133

Collins advertised in 1951 that nearly three million copies of books in the three series had been sold since 1941 and posted to all parts of the world. The tenth anniversary in 1951 coincided with the Festival of Britain and it was decided that the advent of the Festival and the consequent interest of overseas visitors in Britain and the British way of life provided an appropriate time to re-issue 18 of 'the most popular titles'. These were, according to one of the few BIP records retained by Collins:

The English Poets (1) —
Lord David Cecil

English Country Houses (15) —
V. Sackville-West

English Novelists (23) —
Elizabeth Bowen

Life Among the English (31) —
Rose Macaulay

The Birds of Britain (36) —
James Fisher

English Cities and Small Towns (48) —
John Betjeman

Wild Life of Britain (52) —
F. Fraser Darling

British Horses and Ponies (57) —
Lady Wentworth

English Gardens (59) —
Harry Roberts

Wild Flowers in Britain (65) —
Geoffrey Grigson

The English Ballet (80) —
W.J. Turner

Early Britain (92) —
Jacquetta Hawkes

English Cricket (93) —
Neville Cardus

English Glass (99) —
W.B. Honey

The History   37

The English People (100) —   *English Popular and Traditional Art* (102) —
George Orwell   Margaret Lambert and Enid Marx

Roman Britain (113) —   *English Fashion* (121) —
Ian Richmond   Alison Settle

Few of these surprise at being popular, but not all of them were in fact the volumes that sold most copies. According to the figures of sales up to 31 December 1951 recorded by the Company Secretary of Adprint, *Music* (3), *Villages* (11) and *The Story of Scotland* (21), each sold more than 50,000 copies and *Inns* (67), *Postage Stamps* (72) and *Boy Scouts* (75) each sold more than 40,000, but none was chosen for the Festival. Whereas four of the 'most popular' titles that were chosen, namely *People* (100), *Traditional Art* (102), *Roman Britain* (113) and *Fashion* (121), had each sold less than 20,000 copies by the end of 1951. Collins must have used some criteria other than sales when making their selection. On the basis of sales figures up to the end of 1951, the top ten titles were:

The Birds of Britain (36)	— 84,218 —	James Fisher
Life Among the English (31)	— 61,636 —	Rose Macaulay
Wild Flowers in Britain (65)	— 60,574 —	Geoffrey Grigson
The English Poets (1)	— 60,247 —	Lord David Cecil
English Villages (11)	— 56,883 —	Edmund Blunden
Wild Life of Britain (52)	— 56,822 —	F. Fraser Darling
The English Ballet (80)	— 55,975 —	W.J. Turner
English Music (3)	— 52,893 —	W.J. Turner
English Country Houses (15)	— 51,606 —	V. Sackville-West
The Story of Scotland (21)	— 51,105 —	F. Fraser Darling

Sales figures for each volume are recorded in Part 2 together with a commentary on how the figures were compiled. It is perhaps not surprising in a pre-feminist age that Edith Sitwell's book on *English Women* (29) was not among the most popular, selling 19,025 copies, but it does seem surprising that the volume on *British Dogs* (96) at 34,694 was so much less successful than *British Horses* (57) which sold 47,945 copies. Not surprisingly the volumes on political parties, trade unions and hymns did badly, selling between seven and eleven thousand copies each, but those on horse racing, boxing and butterflies did not do much better. Many of these less successful volumes, at least in terms of sales, were published towards the end of the series, their sales perhaps reflecting a gradual lack of momentum and perhaps also exhaustion in the market. Although some of them, for example Vere Temple's *British Butterflies* (125), were among the most beautiful. Collins' total of nearly three million sold was fairly near the mark; excluding omnibus volumes and the Poets series, for which there are no figures, sales to end-1951 totalled 2,793,110 which gives average sales of 24,717 for the 113 British People volumes.

Exact details of the profitability of the series are not known. Representatives of the Publishers' Association who were consulted by Government Ministers and officials estimated in 1942 that a cheap book of the Penguin type would need to sell about 50,000 copies before it was commercially profitable.[1] The BIP books were considerably more expensive than Penguins which retailed at 6d (2½p) each. The price of individual volumes in the People and Commonwealth series rose from 3s 6d (17½p) initially to 4s 6d (22½p) and finally to 5s (25p) at which figure it remained until publication of new volumes ceased in 1950. The Poets series sold at 2s 6d (12½p). Writing to authors in March 1944,[2] Walter Turner stated that 'For some time indeed the series was being worked at a loss to its producers, and it is only during the past twelve months that its success, though limited, has become assured'. Most other books at the time were more expensive; *The Ox-Bow Incident*, a novel, sold in 1941 at 7s 6d (37½p); biographies such as one on James Joyce in that year were 15s (75p); a history by Benedetto Croce sold at 12s 6d (62½p); and a book of engravings of pen-drawings of F.L. Griggs was 52s 6d (£2.62½).[3] At the same time, Walter Turner was being paid £600 a year for a part-time post with the JBC;[4] and the statutory minimum weekly wage of an agricultural worker was £2 8s (£2.40) or nearly £125 a year. In the light of these figures the BIP books do seem very good value and the profit levels not likely to be enormous.

---

[1] Sub-committee on the Supply of Books, 8 July 1942.
[2] Letter of 29 March 1944 to Victoria Sackville-West.
[3] Book prices taken from reviews in *The Times Literary Supplement*.
[4] Walter Turner's salary was recorded in JBC accounts.

WALTER TURNER'S CONTRIBUTION

Much of the 'miracle' referred to by *The Observer* was due to Walter Turner. He valued individuality and creativity above all things and limited his editorial role to ensuring that a subject was properly covered and illustrated. Nevertheless, despite the light editorial hand, there is a coherence in the thought and feeling which pervades many of the volumes. Perhaps this is the result of his selection of authors. Many of them seemed to share a bold and adventurous approach to life, a wide and tolerant culture and that eye for the local, the particular and the domestic, which seems especially British. (The authors, their themes and the quality of their writing are discussed below and biographical details are given in Part 2.) Some impression of Walter Turner's ideas and attitudes can be obtained from one of his last books *Fables, Parables and Plots*, published in 1944. The review in the TLS on 5 February described it as '... a lively mixture of shrewd criticism, poetry and ridicule'. The book is mainly a didactic lecture on banks and money and the absurdity of modern economics. He is concerned about '... the artificial world of scientific devices and manufactured conveniences in which modern man lives ... oblivious of the fundamental realities of nature'. His three volumes of 'autobiography'[1] are romantic and brilliantly original novels in which the experiences of his life, real and imaginary, are transformed into extravagant and delightful fantasies. Writing Turner's entry in *The Dictionary of National Biography*, Jacquetta Hawkes (Mrs J.B. Priestley) refers to the wit, poetic penetration, fantasy, and occasional cussedness of his nature. 'He had', she writes, 'a knowledge of the world, even a kind of ruthlessness, which was yet in perfect harmony with the innocence of a true artist. His poetry is as idiosyncratic as his nature.' For him, BIP was only one of a large number of literary activities, but for the series his contribution was unique and irreplaceable. His sudden death on 18 November 1946 at the age of 57, following a fatal stroke was a catastrophic blow.

Sheila Shannon described him as 'altogether a wonderful man with an invigorating zest for every new experience and an insatiable interest and curiosity in all subjects. He was a very entertaining conversationalist, like Yeats, and the two of them together in the Savile club would talk non-stop, neither appearing to listen to the other. Few people could resist his energetic, impetuous nature.' (Except perhaps Kingsley Martin who sacked him in 1940 without notice after more than twenty years as music critic of the *New Statesman*.) 'I do

---

[1] *Blow For Balloons*, 1935, *Henry Airbubble*, 1936, and *The Duchess of Popocatapetl*, 1939.

W.J. Turner, General Editor of BIP, at the luncheon in the Mayfair Hotel celebrating the publication of the first eight volumes in March 1941.

Sheila Shannon, Assistant General Editor of BIP, in 1942.

not remember any author ever refusing his request to write for BIP. His sudden rages were always directed at things and events, rarely people. He tended to be un-selfcritical, not always able to sort out in his own work what was genius from what was dud. On the other hand, his editorial judgement was admirable, always being generous and constructive in criticism.' Undoubtedly, after Hilda Matheson's initial contribution, he was the driving force behind BIP and when he died so suddenly all impetus was gone. The series was already beginning to run out of steam before his death. 'A large number of subjects had been covered and we did not want to think up others simply to keep things going. The war was over, so the main point of it had disappeared.' There was a relatively small number of books in the pipeline at his death and subsequently each year fewer were published with only nine in 1948 compared with nineteen in the peak years, three in 1949 and one, the last, in 1950. 'Without either the war or Walter there was little point in going on.'

The History　　　　　　　　　　　　　　　　　　　　　　　　　　41

When Walter Turned died in 1946 all his obligations under the contracts passed to his estate; first to his wife Delphine, who survived him by only a year, and then to his nephew, Noel Mewton Wood the brilliant pianist, pupil of Artur Schnabel, who was a lifelong friend of Walter Turner. Mewton Wood committed suicide within a year, his estate passing to his mother in Australia. The business side of BIP was taken over by Adprint, who in 1948 took responsibility for paying royalties to authors and in 1952 paid a lump sum in lieu of all further royalties for copies still in stock at that time. They also presented a complete set of volumes to date to The Princess Elizabeth on the occasion of her marriage.[1] There was one last gasp in 1951 when several volumes were reprinted during the Festival of Britain (see p 36), but BIP had effectively come to an end in 1946.

A MAGNIFICENT ACHIEVEMENT

Subjects

The 113 volumes of 'The British People In Pictures' were grouped into nine main subject areas; History and Achievement (17 volumes), Art and Craftsmanship (19 volumes), Literature and Belles Lettres (10 volumes), Education and Religion (6 volumes), Science, Medicine and Engineering (11 volumes), Social Life and Character (16 volumes), Topographical History (9 volumes), Country Life and Sport (16 volumes) and Natural History (9 volumes). Within these broad categories, details of which are set out in Part 2, an astonishing range of topics was covered. History and Achievement provided an excellent survey of the country's history and its system of Government, beginning with a volume on pre-historic Britain and concluding with three volumes on the main political parties up to the late 1940s. Within this conventional frame, there were also volumes on the more adventurous sides of British life with appropriate emphasis on seamen, soldiers, explorers and, especially important after the Battle of Britain, airmen. Art and Craftsmanship had the largest number of individual volumes. The section covered the traditional arts of music, painting, dance and theatre extremely well and also included fascinating volumes on cartoonists, photographers, furniture makers and popular and traditional art.

[1] Letter of 15 October 1948 from The Princess Elizabeth to Mr Foges.

There were also volumes on postage stamps and books. The section on Literature and Belles Lettres was also fairly catholic, including volumes on orientalists, philosophers and journalists as well as poets, novelists, dramatists, historians, essayists and letter writers. Education and Religion contained fewest volumes, but covered these fields fairly well with especially good volumes on *The English Bible* (66) and *English Hymns and Hymn Writers* (98), the latter in particular being a good example of a title with limited appeal hiding a brilliant essay. Science, Medicine and Engineering contains many fine volumes which display exceptional writing skills as well as deep scientific and engineering knowledge. Social Life and Character shared with Country Life and Sport the second place in number of volumes, but must be fighting for first place in quality with such volumes as that by Edith Sitwell on *English Women* (29), Rose Macaulay's on *Life Among the English* (31) and George Orwell's on *The English People* (100). It is a pity that the planned volumes in this section on conversation and humour were never written, although illustrating them would have posed many difficulties. Country Life and Sport provided some of the most beautiful as well as the most interesting books, including Neville Cardus's lyrical volume on *English Cricket* (93) and Victoria Sackville-West's on *English Country Houses* (15) which was one of the most successful books in the series, being reprinted five times as well as enjoying a special print for the Festival of Britain in 1951. The sections on Topographical History and Natural History provided possibly the best opportunities to the illustrators, and they took them brilliantly.

The seven volumes of the Commonwealth series share the same high qualities as the People series, with especially good ones on *Africa* (*East* (6) and *South* (18)), and *Australia* (5). Considering events in Africa today, the volumes by Elspeth Huxley and Sarah Millin seem especially perceptive; and both books are also exceptionally well written. The Poets series (not to be confused with David Cecil's volume (1)), on the other hand, disappoints; the six volumes are quite unlike the others in format, the small size perhaps being intended to provide poems for the pocket. Whatever the reason, these volumes seem very much an appendage to the BIP series of which they were supposed to be one part. In other respects also they compare unfavourably, having large numbers of misprints, for example. *The Listener*'s review of the launch in 1941 said that 'The third series in this trio seems ... less acceptable than the others. For half a crown[1] we get a mere twenty of Shelley's poems and a few pictures such as Shelley as a Child ... That English poetry should have a prominent shelf in our propaganda

---

[1] 2s 6d in old currency, 12½p in decimal currency.

The History 43

shop-window is an admirable decision, but would not a better notion have been to assemble the poets in quartets, rather than solos?'

Considering the series' stated intention of representing the life, art, institutions and achievements of the British people, it is difficult to think of any glaring omissions. Perhaps the absence of a volume devoted to the Monarchy seems surprising, as does one specifically devoted to soccer. The church, army and medicine were covered, but not law. The cinema, then reaching its peak, was not recorded, but the great days of British cinema were perhaps in the years after the war, which was the time when BIP was declining.

1939-45 War

The war was not covered by a specific volume. According to Sheila Shannon, as the aim was to show what Britain had achieved in major areas of life, a particular war or aspect of that war, however important, would be too limited a subject. However, the subject could not be avoided and there were references to the war in many of the volumes. G. M. Young, himself a contributor to the series (4), suggested when reviewing another volume that the evacuation of children from London and other cities vulnerable to bombing would provide a good subject; and it was covered very well in the volume on *Women's Institutes* (61) by Cicely McCall. Her description of the arrival of evacuees in the countryside, their initial idealistic reception, and the later horror-struck realisation of the problems of dealing with dirty, verminous, ill-fed, badly clothed and extremely 'street-wise' children, is a delight to read. It is also a valuable historical document as it was written in 1941-42 when the evacuations had recently taken place and was based on accounts sent in to WI headquarters by local Institutes. It is a careful account which tries very hard to be fair, but there is no disguising the great shock as one Britain faced another, quite different, Britain. It was town facing country, poverty facing relative prosperity, sophistication facing simplicity, in short, one tribal culture facing another, not casually, but in close and continuing contact. This volume certainly gave real insights into Britain in the 1940s and the British character. The WI had helped in the organisation of the evacuation, but had some difficulty otherwise in developing a war-time role. The organisation was non-political and non-sectarian and had to accommodate a variety of views ranging from the militantly aggressive to the pacifism of Quaker members. As late as June 1939 at their annual conference delegates felt able to give a rapturous welcome to the delegate from Germany and the emotional scenes are well described in the book. In the end the WI found a fairly non-contentious war-time role by means of jam. A glut of fruit in 1940 prompted a great voluntary effort by the Institutes which, using sugar provided by their Headquarters, preserved 1,631 tons of fruit. In the following year this voluntary effort was supported by Government as part of the rationing of food, and jam was to become, rather unfairly, almost a symbol of the WI movement for most people. Sylvia Lynd in her volume on *English Children* (30) used an oil painting by B. Fleetwood-Walker of children evacuated to the country and tells a brief anecdote about an evacuee in her final paragraphs.

One of the most graphic descriptions of the war appears in the most unlikely volume of all, that on *The English Ballet* (80), with its eye witness report (already referred to on p 13) of the escape of The Sadler's Wells company from Holland in May 1940 after the German invasion of that country. There are illustrations of London in the blitz in *The Londoner* (64) and *British Photographers* (71), of St Thomas's Hospital in war time in *British Hospitals* (131), of people queueing for fish in *The English People* (100) and one of the weekly food ration for a family of two in *The English at Table* (51). Several authors linked their themes to some aspect of the war, for example Edmund Blunden in *English Villages* (11) reporting a pub conversation about the shortage of beer; Robert McNair Wilson in *British Medicine* (12) recording the loss by bombing of a priceless collection of anatomical specimens built up by William Hunter the eighteenth century surgeon; and John Betjeman in *English Cities and Small Towns* (48) pointing out that even bombing had its silver linings as it removed much ugly stained glass and unwanted woodwork.

An ominous aspect to the war which was not, of course, apparent from the books, was the fact that many of the authors would not have survived a German invasion. For example, David Low who wrote *British Cartoonists, Caricaturists and Comic Artists* (25) had been reliably informed that he had been included in the Gestapo list for elimination because of his anti-fascist cartoons.[1]

The war even found its way into *The Birds of Britain* (36) where James Fisher records that as he writes in midsummer 1942 '... intelligence comes of black redstarts in several English towns; of about twelve singing males in central London ... (where) ornithologists are seeking nests in the blitzed city, and among the ruins of the burnt-out Guildhall.' Another fascinating picture of life during the war was drawn by Rose Macaulay in *Life Among the English* (31). 'Bets were taken on the date of the war ... Britain became bomb conscious: trenches were dug; many Londoners went to earth in the country; ... windows were criss-crossed with tape; gas masks were carried about and left in cinemas and on blackberry bushes, bags of sand lay on pavements, rotted, sprouted, and

---

[1] Article by D. Pepys-Whitely in DNB.

The History

burst asunder; through cimmerian blackness torches were flashed, annoying drivers; women went into trousers, civilians into fire, ambulance and wardens' stations, older men into the Home Guard; young men and women were put into the forces and factories, enemy aliens (hostile and friendly) into camps, British Fascists and others into gaol, policemen into tin hats. Cars crashed all night into street refuges, pedestrians and each other; the warning banshee wailed by night and day; people left their beds and sat in shelters and knitted balaclava helmets. Bombs tore homes to pieces; some (if they had survived this catastrophe), took fresh homes, others were surprised to find how well they got on without homes, sleeping in shelters, where a cheerful, if at times malicious, envious and quarrelsome social life throve . . .' and much more in like vein.

Perhaps the most powerful and beautiful image linking the theme of a volume to the time in which it was written, is in the concluding paragraph of (Dame) Veronica Wedgwood's book on *Battlefields in Britain* (78):

> Culloden Moor, the scene of this last and final defeat of the Celtic north by the Anglo-Saxon, is a site as beautiful as it is tragic, with the desolate moor under a wild sky and the long graves of the clans buried in the places where they fell. With it the tale of fighting on British soil comes to an end, to re-open in a different element close on two hundred years later, when those few who, in the skies above this island saved the civilisation of the world, outfought and outmanoeuvred the German attack and 'left the quivering air signed with their honour'.[1]

Illustrations

Edmund Blunden in his introduction to the omnibus volume *The Englishman's Country* (135), commented on 'the remarkable array of British artists who, . . . dead or living, contribute so well to the volume.' The same comment could justly be applied to the whole series. For this record alone of British artists, BIP deserves to be remembered. In 126 books there were 1,040 colour plates and 2,869 black-and-white illustrations. The books contain an excellent record of British illuminated manuscripts, portraits, prints, drawings and paintings of all kinds. Given the title of the series, the illustrations had to be a significant part of the book and the space provided for them was not very much less than that for the words. The full-page colour illustrations, of which there were usually eight (sometimes twelve or four) pages, were always additional to the 48 numbered pages. Taking account of five pages for the half-title, advertisement, title,

---

[1] The source is probably Stephen Spender's 1909 poem 'I think continually of those who were truly great' which ends with the words 'And left the vivid air signed with their honour'.

printer's imprint, and lists of illustrations, and between 11 to 33 black-and-white illustrations, the space available for text usually amounted to about 30 pages, sufficient only for 12-14,000 words. The 48 page limit was exceeded on only six occasions, three of which, perhaps unsurprisingly, were the volumes about the main political parties.

Walter Turner was very keen not to use photographs as illustrations except when it was appropriate to do so, as for *British Photographers* (71) by Cecil Beaton. This was mainly because he wanted to show the range of British art, although an additional consideration was that photography was mainly associated with newspapers, and with magazines such as *Picture Post*. At first he had hoped that all the books might be illustrated by twentieth century artists, providing a record of the best of modern British art, but this became less practicable and appropriate as the series was developed. Extensive use was made, however, of the work of modern artists, including some just beginning to establish their high reputations. Some of the authors also included their own paintings or drawings, for example, Vere Temple in her book on *British Butterflies* (125) and Peter Bicknell in *British Hills and Mountains* (116). The decision to make maximum use of paintings and drawings meant, first, deciding on the ones to use, and then finding out where they had been stored. Many paintings had been removed from galleries and private collections to the country for safety. The links with Government were especially useful in gaining access to these hidden treasures. Museums, galleries, private collections and individual owners were the sources of paintings and drawings, and curators and owners were generous in helping a project that showed the riches of Britain then under threat. Among other fascinating jobs, visits to caves above Aberystwyth, where many of the drawings from the British Museum were stored, became necessary for Walter Turner and Sheila Shannon, accompanied by John Hinde who worked for Adprint, and would photograph the paintings and drawings *in situ* as none was allowed to be moved. This presented all sorts of problems, not least being that of sufficient light. Compromises had to be made both in the selection of illustrations and in the quality of reproduction.[1]

Reviewers of the books were usually complimentary about the illustrations, but there were occasions when a more critical assessment was offered, particularly about the relationship between the words and pictures. *The Listener*'s reviewer of *English Music* (3) on 20 March 1941 wrote that 'The job of illustrating such a series as this is a difficult one. Mr Turner had evidently been at

---

[1] Account based on discussion with Sheila Shannon. John Hinde subsequently started a business producing postcards.

his wit's end to find a dozen pictures in colour appropriate to a potted history of English Music. No fewer than five of the twelve turn out to be variations on that most hackneyed of portrait painter themes, the So-and-So family playing string quartettes in the drawing room. The black-and-white illustrations, mostly of famous scores or celebrated composers are much more vivid and interesting, and also easier on the eye than the luscious hues of most of the colour-plates.' Many of the issues and difficulties involved in selecting illustrations, were considered in a letter of 3 July 1943 from the historian E. S. De Beer who commented on the TLS review of E. L. Woodward's book on *British Historians* (49):

> It is to be regretted that in your review ... very little attention is paid to the illustrations. In books in such a series as to that which it belongs one hopes to find the illustrations an integral part of the text, not treated as a more or less pleasant adjunct to it; selected by the author, just as documents of any other kind would be, to enrich his argument and to advance it through a second medium. Further, one expects a high degree of accuracy in the description of the reproduction.
>
> The illustrations in Mr Woodward's book fall into two groups. On the one hand there are the portraits of historians, views of places associated with them, and illustrations derived from the original or early editions of their works; on the other more or less fanciful pictures of historical events and miscellaneous views. The relevance of this second group is questionable: Mr Woodward does not discuss the development of the representation of historical events; nor is there a sufficient number of pictures in this group to show the development by themselves; those that there are are not arranged in a proper sequence for this purpose (one may note further that some of the events represented are not mentioned in the text). With some exceptions the selection of subjects in the first group is excellent; the illustrations from Mathew Paris and Holinshed are particularly attractive, as well as some of the portraits.

Professor De Beer went on to criticise particular illustrations, and to point out some inaccurate ascriptions. He concluded:

> Publishers cannot as a rule be expected to know the special problems and the materials available for appropriate illustration; if standards are to be raised authors and reviewers must give the matter the attention it deserves.

Such comments about relating illustrations to the text were, rightly, echoed in some other reviews. Rex Warner's book on *English Public Schools* (90), for example, was criticised for the fact that the illustrations fail '... to convey any clear impression of either the development or the nature of the English Public School.' The illustrations in *The English People* (100) '... are plentiful and good, but not many have any close relationship to Mr Orwell's text.' Perhaps it was rather easier for Geoffrey Grigson whose illustrations for *Wild Flowers in*

Britain (65) were thought to be '... very beautiful and have a historical flavour in pleasant harmony with the text.' Sometimes, the illustrations, although acknowledged as good, were simply overwhelmed by the quality of the writing. The TLS reviewer thought that the illustrations in *English Cricket* (93) '... cannot begin to compare with the interest of Mr Cardus's prose.' One of the more successful marriages of words and pictures is in Janet Adam Smith's volume on *Children's Illustrated Books* (126) where pictures nearly always link up exactly with text. Perhaps she took special care to do so in view of her observation on children's books that their readers '... clearly love the picture that really illustrates, that chimes in every detail with the text'. Other volumes also produced similarly happy results, that on *British Postage Stamps* (72), for example, where it is difficult to find a significant reference that is not illustrated or an illustration that is not referred to in the text. Peter Bicknell when preparing his *British Hills and Mountains* (116) worked hard on making sure that his fine selection of illustrations was related specifically to the text, but editorial policy did not allow him either to have references in the text or explanatory captions under the pictures. Authors varied a great deal in the amount of interest they took in the selection of illustrations. Usually the relevance of the illustrations was highly praised and in general there was a good balance between words and pictures.[1]

The quality of reproduction of the illustrations was also usually commended, for example those in *The Story of Wales* (62), *South Africa* (18), *British Mountaineers* (22), *The Story of Scotland* (21), *British Hills and Mountains* (116) and many, many others deservedly received high praise. Miss Enid Marx, who co-authored *English Popular and Traditional Art* (24) with Margaret Lambert, and is herself a notable artist, commented on the very high quality of reproduction, expressing the view that colour reproduction had made little progress, in popular books at least, since 'Britain In Pictures'.[2] The quality of reproduction in most of the volumes is staggeringly high, especially when one bears in mind the conditions of scarcity and other difficulties under which they were produced, but there were some criticisms. The reproduction process '... is unkind to line blocks, coarsening Bewick in a way which only comparison with the originals will show' according to John Rayner who reviewed *The Birds of Britain* (36) in *The Observer* of 6 December 1942. The following week their review of John Piper's *British Romantic Artists* (34) ended by expressing disappointment that he had included no example of his own work, adding rather

---

[1] Comments taken from reviews and Peter Bicknell letter of 18 June 1994.
[2] Miss Marx gave me her views in August 1993.

spitefully that '... it must be admitted, after glancing at the colour reproductions that his modesty is understandable.' *The Listener*'s reviewer disagreed: 'In appearance alone, his book is perhaps the best that has yet appeared in the BIP series, in which the reproductions have not pleased all the people all the time. Among the coloured plates, landscapes by Cotman, Samuel Palmer and F. Danby ... and an industrial scene by Graham Sutherland call for particular note, and there are pretty reproductions in monochrome works by, among others, Cozens, Bewick, John Martin, Pinwell and Ford Madox Brown.' The most successful reproductions are obviously those of engravings, lithographs and line drawings which were intended for reproduction in books and magazines. Aquatints come out very well and plates of birds, mammals, insects and plants are almost always of a very high standard. Reproductions of oil paintings are mixed in quality. The TLS reviewer referred disparagingly to '... the chocolate-box plate of a pink-and-white waxwork ...' which purported to be King George V in G.M. Young's volume on *The Government of Britain* (4). The colours in some of the oil reproductions seem dull, with shades that are unlikely to be found in the originals. Difficulties encountered in photographing originals during the war have already been described.

John Piper, reviewing a book in another contemporary series, one of the 'King Penguin' books, in March 1941, wrote that '... many of the (colour reproductions) look like a mess on the bathroom linoleum.' This is not unlike Ralph Burdon's reaction when he first saw the volume on *New Zealand* (26) which he had written with Ngaio Marsh; his daughter wrote that on seeing the cover he said that it looked as if Maoris had taken over the Harris Tweed factory. Reflecting on the difficulties of reproducing paintings, John Piper wrote that he had come to the conclusion that 'Clarity of colour and sharpness of outline (in the originals) are all. The successful ones were painted in flat colours tied together with good black lines.' None of the BIP volumes could fairly be described as a mess, but the truth of Mr Piper's analysis is borne out by the most successful reproductions. There was not, in the 1940s and earlier, in Britain, much experience of producing cheap, high quality, illustrated books. The series was fortunate in having the assistance of those emigrés from Austria, already referred to, in particular Wolfgang Foges, with his obsession for popularising colour illustration, and Walter Neurath who directed the design team and was responsible for the high quality of reproduction.

Authors and their Writing

There were 117 authors in all, of whom seven wrote two books each and six wrote three books jointly. Dorothy Wellesley edited the six volumes of the Poets series and Walter Turner, as well as being general editor for the three series, wrote two of the volumes in the People series and edited all seven of the omnibus volumes. Of the 117 authors, 22 were women. As indicated earlier (p27), all authors were paid the same and joint authors had to share the payment; in 1942 Ngaio Marsh wrote to Ralph Burdon 'In the end you have written about half this book and when it is all over I shall have great pleasure in presenting you with half its paltry payment'.[1]

It is almost impossible to generalise about the variety of authors. Several of the contributors were professional novelists or poets, for example Graham Greene, Elizabeth Bowen, George Orwell, John Betjeman, Kate O'Brien, Edmund Blunden, Rose Macaulay and Edith Sitwell. Even if the essay was not their customary form of writing, they were bound to produce something worthwhile. Similarly, journalists such as Neville Cardus, Bernard Darwin, Derek Hudson and Denzil Batchelor, were professional writers and seemed very comfortable with the restriction of 12-14,000 words, although compared to most of their writing this would have been a fairly generous allowance. Academics, such as G.M. Young or E.L. Woodward, more accustomed to ampler space in which to express themselves, might have felt more restricted, but none of them showed any signs of this in their essays. There is a 'quirkiness' about some of the choices of author. Why Graham Greene to write about dramatists, for example? Apart from writing novels, his other main work at the time was cinema criticism. He made several abortive attempts at playwriting, but achieved no success until 1952 with 'The Living Room'. Nevertheless, his book on *British Dramatists* (32) demonstrated that he was an inspired choice for this subject. Why Rhys Davies for *The Story of Wales* (62), unless to provoke the Welsh? His carnal tales were not likely to have endeared him to Welshmen, at least in North Wales — reviewers commented on his southern bias. We should be grateful, however, for his having been chosen, if only for his delightful description of Dr William Price of Llantrisant who lived from 1800 to 1893 and in a lifetime which ranged across English Victorianism and Welsh puritanism nevertheless succeeded in pioneering cremation, nudism and free love and maintained the lifestyle of a vegetarian whose favourite drink was champagne.

---
[1] Burdon correspondence op cit.

One of the strengths of the series is how these short books included not only the established names of British history and culture, but also the minor figures and eccentrics such as Dr Price. Kate O'Brien writing about *English Diaries and Journals* (55) of course comments on Evelyn, Pepys and Parson Woodforde, but also includes the writings of William Windham, Miss Weeton, Benjamin Haydon and Henry Crabbe Robinson. In S.H.F. Johnston's *British Soldiers* (50) the reader can hear not only Marlborough and Wellington, but also the officers and the men; small wars are described as well as great; and garrison duties get their due account as well as battles. Major Johnston, who was an academic as well as a soldier, can convey the drama and excitement of fighting without ignoring either the horrors, or the tedious details of organisation and supply, which underlie most great victories. Almost any volume picked at random displays this comprehensive quality, all the more impressive for confining it within 48 pages.

Most of the writers came from professional and upper-middle class backgrounds, with a sprinkling from the aristocratic and working classes. Sir Ernest Barker, who wrote *British Statesmen* (13), was the son of a coal-miner. Sir Richard Gregory, the author of *British Scientists* (14) and the greatest scientific journalist of his day, started work at the age of 12, first as a newspaper boy and then as a clicker in a boot and shoe factory. This early start in working life was shared by (Lord) Citrine, who began to teach himself to become an electrician when he left elementary school at the age of 12 before taking on the trade union work which led him to the General Secretaryship of the Trades Union Congress, the Chairmanship of the Central Electricity Authority and the authorship of *British Trade Unions* (45). Other backgrounds were less hard, but no less unusual. The man who wrote the volume on *Australia* (5), Arnold Haskell, was a ballet director who became Director of the Royal Ballet School and obtained his Australian credentials after a visit to Australia in 1936 to accompany and report on the Russian Ballet tour. Lady Wentworth was 60 when she wrote *British Horses and Ponies* (57) and had by then become a world recognised expert on horse breeding. She had also been World Lady Royal Tennis champion, a game that was not then regarded as suitable for women, and a poet and painter. She sat for Burne-Jones who was entranced by her 'perfect beauty combined with the speed and lightness of foot of some wild creature.' In her independence of mind, her eccentricities, her artistic pursuits, and her stormy domestic relations she reflected her ancestry, both her father William Scawen Blunt and her maternal great-grandfather Lord Byron. 'A character as strong as hers could hardly keep out of controversy; indeed, like the biblical war-horse which she loved so much, she probably smelled the battle from afar and she was a doughty opponent.'[1] She survived her book to fight on for another 13 years. Thomas Hennell, on the other hand, had scarcely finished his book on *British Craftsmen* (38) before he left for an assignment as a British war artist in South-East Asia, was captured by Indonesian nationalists, taken into the jungle, and never seen again.[2] The authors who contributed to BIP are admirable, not only for their excellent books, but also for their lives. If Walter Turner knew even a half of them, he must have enjoyed a rich existence indeed. (There is a list of authors in Part 2 and brief biographical details are given in the Chronological List together with information on their volume.)

The series published many dazzling essays and the best of them, like all good essays, were those which recognised the need for a comprehensive approach to their subject, but managed by clever use of themes to avoid being swamped by detail. Writing about the history and procedures of *The House of Commons* (117), (Sir) Martin Lindsay MP succeeded in providing an historical retrospect in ten pages which seems not to have omitted anything of importance, and this is the largest section of the book! This skill in handling large themes was shared by many of the other authors. In *British Romantic Artists* (34) John Piper so compressed and illuminated his subject that '... the result is not a mere outline (he contrives to mention painters as diverse as W.J. Muller, James Smetham and Ivon Hitchins) but an exquisite and valuable essay.' Elspeth Huxley's volume on *East Africa* (6) was described as a model of intelligent Empire propaganda: 'Although she has only 12,000 words for her job, Mrs Huxley never seems to lack elbow room; and not only does she narrate the history, the tribal life, the trade and the administrative organisation of East Africa, but she finds room also for some candid references to many colonial problems which have still to be solved. Arnold Haskell's *Australia* (5) is almost as good, and his pictures, like Mrs Huxley's, are admirably chosen and well produced.' One of the most impressive volumes of the whole series is Professor Sir Ernest Barker's on *British Statesmen* (13); '... in small compass he has treated it with remarkable skill, packing into a few pages a great deal of wisdom, drawing from examples permanent principles, and withal so handling the matter that nothing he says is for a moment above the understanding of ordinary man.' This was the view of the TLS reviewer and there were similarly appreciative reviews for other historical essays such as Dame Veronica Wedgwood's *Battlefields in Britain* (78) and Jacquetta Hawkes' *Early Britain* (92).[3]

[1] Quotations from *The Times* obituary 10 August 1957.
[2] Disappearance of Thomas Hennell in Vol 3 of J. Rothenstein's *Modern British Painters* pub Macdonald 1952.
[3] Quotations are from reviews, for dates of which see entry in chronological list.

The History

The least successful of the essays were those which were little more than a chronology of events. One of these is the Bishop of Chichester's essay on *The English Church* (28). The reviewer's judgement was harsh: 'Valuable as is the detailed information given, it cannot be said that there emerges a picture of what the essential genius of the Church of England is, such as might kindle the imagination.' Some of the books which had fascinating subjects, such as David Low's *Cartoonists, Caricaturists and Comic Artists* (25) or *Fairs, Circuses and Music Halls* (46) by M. Willson Disher, turn out to be much less entertaining than the title leads one to expect. Whereas others with much less promising titles, such as *British Ports and Harbours* (35) by Leo Walmsley or Mettius Chappell's *British Engineers* (47) are lively and amusing to read. In *Life Among the English* (31), Rose Macaulay demonstrated how to tackle in a short essay so big and diffuse a subject. She began confidently: 'Owing to the weather, English Social life must always have largely occurred either indoors, or, when out of doors, in active motion.' She went on to divide her subject into seven periods, but as the TLS reviewer said she '... has resisted (if she ever felt it) the temptation to allot to each of these periods a text-book character and selection does not seem to have hampered her free movement among the matters that have occurred to her as interesting.'

Many of the books, like Rose Macaulay's, start off with a good first sentence. Edith Sitwell asserted that 'The distinguishing quality of the English is character, not intellect ...', a provocative opening for any essay, but especially so for the one on *English Women* (29). Her book provoked some lively correspondence in the TLS in June and July 1942 when she so exasperated one reader that he was reduced to saying '... she swerves and side-steps with the ease and assurance of a crack centre three quarter'. John Gilmour writing on *British Botanists* (79) began with diffident charm that 'Botany is perhaps the least sensational of sciences ...'. Opening *British Medicine* (12), R. McNair Wilson was more aggressive and claimed that 'The English, contrary to general belief, are the most scientifically minded of all peoples, and so careful and exact in their observation that medical progress owes more to them than to any other race of mankind.' Kate O'Brien, writing *English Diaries and Journals* (55) begins by saying that '... the best English diaries have been written by bores.' Nearly all the essays capture the attention with the first words, and hold it thereafter with interesting ideas expressed in good, clear English.

In some of the books the style is less a matter of wit or fine writing than a powerful reflection of the knowledge and direct experience of the writer. Several of the authors had lived through many of the events they were describing. Admiral Sir Edward Evans, for example, who wrote the volume on

British Polar Explorers (53), forty years earlier, in 1902, had been selected to be Second Officer of 'The Morning', the relief ship sent out by the Royal Geographical Society to the first Antarctic expedition of R. F. Scott. In 1909 he was selected by Scott himself as second in command of his second expedition and Captain of 'The Terra Nova' which left England in 1910. He accompanied Scott in January 1912 to within 150 miles of the Pole before having to return, desperately ill. His essay reflects this direct experience and his tough, straightforward, no-nonsense character: 'In these pages you will find a simple sailor's appreciation of his favourite squires and knights of the Polar Seas'. This was the 'simple sailor' who captained 'The Broke' which rammed one of six German destroyers when it was bombarding Dover harbour in April 1917. In 1933, when Commander in Chief on the African Station, he deposed the Chief of the Bamangwoto tribe who had flogged a European man for assaulting an African woman, and then proceeded to expel the European; he did this when only temporarily acting as High Commissioner in the absence of Sir John Stanley. He remained active in the Second War, being appointed as Winston Churchill's personal emissary to the King of Norway when that country was invaded and later acted as London Regional Defence Commissioner. This was the 'simple sailor' who wrote in the Foreword to his BIP volume that 'It seems only a few months ago since I felt that strong, sincere hand-shake from Captain Oates ... when my part in the longest sledge journey on record had been played and I bowed and went my way.' As the TLS reviewer wrote 'Physical penetration of a subject can hardly go deeper than this'. *British Mountaineers* (22) was written by F. S. Smythe who, when invalided out of the RAF in 1927, was advised that for the rest of his life when walking upstairs he should go slowly. Instead, he took up mountaineering and was a member of three Everest expeditions in 1933, '36 and '38, having previously in 1931 conquered Mt Kamet, the first peak over 25,000ft ever to be climbed. Mr Smythe was perhaps more sure-footed climbing mountains than in proof reading, but the number of minor slips detected by the TLS reviewer in the text does not detract at all from the authority and excitement of the story. Many of the slips had already been noted by him in a letter to Sheila Shannon written on 15 May 1942 which also provides a moving demonstration of the difficulties of the time:

> I owe you and Mr Turner my sincere congratulations and thanks for the beautiful production of British Mountaineers. I would have written before but I've been away on RAF duties and am only now attending to accumulated correspondence. You have taken great pains with the illustrations. Everyone is enchanted by them. One small thing — you have probably been told that the pictures of Leslie Stephen and Prof

Forbes have their titles reversed. A pity I didn't see the titled pulls. Also 'Sixteenth Century' on page 8 should read 'Eighteenth Century'.

I think people appreciate hills more now than at any time because the sales of my books are phenomenal — though the difficulty is paper is great (sic). My publishers lost about 10,000 volumes at Stationers' Hall and elsewhere in the city bombing. I long to write and see the hill(s) and can only live in hopes that the old Polish prophecy which has come true in every detail so far will continue to come true. If so, Poland is a free nation when Easter falls on St Mark's day — and that is in April 1943.

There are writers who seem since the 1940s to have been forgotten, but whose BIP volume makes one impatient to read more of their work. Sarah Millin, the South African novelist and historian, displayed in her book on *South Africa* (18) an awe-inspiring directness and economy of writing. *The Times* obituarist in July 1968 referred to her '... clear, clenched prose, with never a word wasted ...' Her BIP volume displays this quality to the full. Another prose stylist of distinction was Leo Walmsley whose *British Ports and Harbours* (35) opens with an evocation of a childhood in Whitby that is almost Dickensian in its power and humour. His writing, like that of Sarah Millin and other BIP authors, deserves to be better known.

Almost any one of the books could be selected to demonstrate the high quality of the writing and the essential characteristics of the series. *British Philosophers* (68) by Kenneth Matthews, is a good example to take. The subject is inherently difficult for a popular series, especially one which also imposed a limit of 48 pages for each book. The TLS reviewer commented '... It is obvious that in the short space of fifty (sic) pages there was no alternative before Mr Matthews but to leave gaps and suppress many worthy names', and he is to be congratulated in having succeeded, in spite of the handicap, in giving a well-proportioned and clear conspectus of his subject down to the time of Mill, including a treatment of Hobbes, Locke, Berkeley and Hume which could hardly be improved upon in so short a compass ...'.[1] The reviewer goes on to complain about one or two omissions of his own favourites, but Mr Matthews passes the first test triumphantly — his book is lucid and comprehensive, even bringing the common reader right up to date with a brief account of modern philosophy, including the influence of psychology and the new physics. The book never becomes a mere list. Into his comprehensive account he wove a number of interesting themes, including the provocative one introduced in his first arresting sentence: 'Two major influences have shaped the philosophy of modern Europe: the British and the German.' Using this particular theme, rather a sensitive one in 1943 when

[1] TLS 26 February 1944.

the two countries were at war, he is able to take the reader immediately into the general subject in a fascinating way.

The writing is brilliant. Almost every sentence is a model of clear, vigorous and elegant prose. Three quotations will have to suffice as examples:

> The British philosophers, at least the most typical of them, stand with both feet on the ground. They are, compared with the great German system builders, Kant, Hegel, Leibnitz and others, earthbound and pedestrian figures. But then, they would say, a sound philosophy is a utility product, which must be capable of taking hard knocks.
>
> But when a philosophy erected like Kant's or Hegel's, tier upon tier of abstract superstructure upon a pinpoint of experience, falls out of fashion, it falls like Lucifer, never to rise again.
>
> ... common sense is not a dull quality. Rather the contrary. Nothing is more calculated to shock people than common sense applied to long established but unexamined beliefs. This was the indiscretion which long ago put a cup of hemlock in front of Socrates.[1]

The British/German antithesis is never conducted in any jingoistic tone. This too is generally characteristic of the writing in the series. Obviously all the books represent British achievement, partly as a matter of record in case the worst happened and the country was invaded or even defeated, and partly as a matter of pride. There is a distinctively British flavour to each of them, but they are never bombastic and do not disparage other nations. The criticism in *British Philosophers* of some German contributions to philosophy, is offered in a cool, academic, philosophical way. It stimulated a leader in the TLS which took up the theme: '... our unbending resolve to crush utterly the barbaric power into which Germany has transformed herself must not blind us to the achievements of German thought in the days when Germany still lived within the Christian and humane traditions of Europe. Then the Rhine did, as was said, "flow into the Thames", and the Thames was not defiled by it.'[2] This tolerant and judicious approach is shared by the authors of the series, although all of them usually managed to avoid the slightly pompous tone of voice so characteristic of newspapers and journals of the 1940s.

Finally, *British Philosophers* was a challenge to the illustrators. Inevitably, and not inappropriately in view of the subject, much use was made of portraits — there are fourteen. One of them, Roger Fry's oil painting of J.M.E. M'Taggart, reproduces especially well, thus overcoming the usual difficulties in

---

[1] Quotations are from pp 7 and 8.
[2] TLS 26 February 1944.

reproducing that medium.[1] The other illustrations are of places associated with particular philosophers or more generally with philosophy, although rather loosely it must be admitted; and there is a reproduction of the title page of Hobbes' *Leviathan*. The volume demonstrates the difficulties in illustrating adequately some subjects, but also a large degree of success in overcoming them. *British Philosophers* is not the best of all the books in the series; some of the others have better illustrations and the volumes by Rose Macaulay (31), Edmund Blunden (11), Victoria Sackville-West (15), Sarah Millin (18) and many more are all brilliantly written. It is, however, a good example of the whole, being above all a brilliant essay which demonstrates those qualities of brevity, clarity and wit to explain and illuminate an important subject which were so characteristic of the series.

Critics' Reception

The main periodicals of the time reviewed the series favourably. *The Times Literary Supplement* reviewed carefully almost every volume and often used an illustration from one of the books on its front page. *The Observer* was enthusiastic and continued to keep a benign eye on the series until the end, although it did not review every volume. *The Spectator* and *The Listener* both noted favourably the launch of the series and reviewed occasional volumes. The *New Statesman and Nation*, like *The Times*, did not report its launch and neither seem to have reviewed the books regularly. Paper restrictions at the time mean that it is not possible to read any real significance into this as many periodicals complained that they did not have sufficient space for reviews.

WHAT SORT OF BRITAIN — OR ENGLAND?

One curious feature of many of the volumes is the way in which the words 'Britain' and 'England', 'British' and 'English', were used. The series is about the 'British' people, although its first statement of aims begins with 'The English'! (See p 29). Sometimes the word 'English' was used specifically and properly to define the precise limits of the study, as in *English Rivers and Canals* (84), because the authors knew little about rivers or canals in Wales, Scotland or Ireland. Whilst the distinction was sometimes used deliberately in this way in order to limit the scope of the study, more usually it seems to have been part of that

---

[1] Roger Fry's portrait of M'Taggart is opposite p 41 of *British Philosophers* (68).

Anglocentric convention that for 'England' one should, of course, read also Wales, Scotland and Ireland. This no doubt explains why there were British dramatists, but only English poets; British Philosophers, but only English novelists. Of the 132 numbered volumes, a total of 63 had Britain or British in the title and 35 England or English, the remaining 34 referring to neither. There was usually a totally unselfconscious use of England to mean Britain, even by Scottish authors such as Robert McNair Wilson. Only the author of *British Ships and Ship Builders* (104), George Blake, writing after the war in 1946 as the series was coming to an end, felt '... that we have to be careful nowadays how we use the terms English and British.' Perhaps this was one of the signs of the new post-war age which was to be rather different from the centuries described in so many of the BIP volumes; a change in mood and outlook also picked up in another way by Christopher Marsden in his 1947 volume on *The English at the Seaside* (112) when he suggested '... that when the fission bombs are on the move you might just as well be at the seaside as anywhere else.'

The sort of Britain shown in the books was very far from a nuclear age, but the general picture was not at all that of the rural, genteel or tourist brochure Britain which other contemporary series, such as *Recording Britain*, sometimes tended to show. Perhaps this is because topography, landscape and architecture form only a small part of BIP. Also perhaps because most of the authors take a fairly hard-headed approach to life as illustrated by their attitudes towards country life and industrialisation. The countryside is important, but not treated reverentially. First, it was the location of political power; both the landowner Guy Paget (87) and the radical writer George Orwell (100) point out that the real homes of the ruling classes in Britain are in the country and not in the capital. Even in *Roman Britain* (113), according to Dr Ian Richmond, the native aristocracy were suspicious of the metropolis and preferred to keep their wealth and families in the country. Associated with this preference for the country rather than the capital was a widespread suspicion of centralisation and a general assumption that it was better for decisions to be dispersed between a large number of localities and self-governing institutions rather than concentrated in London. Many of the writers warned of threats to the quality of life from the growth of cities and centralisation of power.

They warned also against some contemporary developments in farming and the destruction of wild-life, flora and fauna. It is sobering to read The Earl of Portsmouth's book, *British Farm Stock* (132), the last of the series published in 1950, with its concerns about factory farming methods, its criticism of excessive specialisation in farming, and the danger foreseen of increased disease from, for example, specialised egg farms. The approach of BIP writers, however, was different from that of environmentalists today. None of the naturalists and countrylovers writing for BIP wanted to return to a pre-industrial age; they welcomed industrialisation and saw no incompatibility between the introduction of modern conveniences and a good environment. F. Fraser Darling, Geoffrey Grigson and C. M. Yonge were sceptical about the 'naturalness' of the natural world and demonstrated how much of what we describe as 'nature' is in fact attributable to the activities of people. So there is little sentimentality in their vision of rural life and most of the writers take a realistic view about its virtues and vices.

Similarly, those authors writing about art and design usually welcomed modern developments such as the introduction of machines. Few of them ache for a rural idyll of handicrafts; good design and craftsmanship are not seen as incompatible with an industrial society. Michael Ayrton in *British Drawings* (105) complained of '... the second black death, the industrial materialism of Victorian Times', but it was materialistic attitudes that he rejected, not machines. John Gloag in *British Furniture Makers* (89) was emphatic that '... machinery and mass production need not destroy taste', an opinion shared by Thomas Hennell in *British Craftsmen* (38), Lady Sempill in *English Pottery and China* (77) and Enid Marx and Margaret Lambert in *English Popular and Traditional Art* (24). All of them detect a significant change of taste in Victorian times, but they attributed this to the dominance of the moneyed middle class, not to the introduction of capitalism or machines. Thus they differed from some contemporary Marxist trends of thought which linked matters of taste to the means of production.

Edmund Blunden in his *English Villages* (11) thought that all might be well if England were now '... planned as a whole', but most of the authors would have disagreed and shared instead the opinion of the TLS reviewer of *English Villages* (11) who thought that '... any planning today will be more like Dagenham than Bath, for who can escape the spirit of the age.' Running through most of the books was the conviction that individuals produced great art, good taste and a pleasant environment, not the technologies that happened to be available to them. Most of the volumes eschew ideology and concentrate on individuals and their achievements, giving an over-riding impression of rich variety, vigour, inventiveness, courage, boldness and individuality. It is significant that this British propaganda response to the clash of ideologies in the war emphasised freedom and individuality, not any competing social or government theories and systems.

The Britain that is shown is quite different from today; it was a nation of localities, private institutions and distinct communities, not a national conglomorate; it preferred modest, amateur delights rather than professional activities with mass-appeal; above all, it elevated the individual above the state.

In her introduction to the omnibus volume which contains seven of the volumes related to English literature (134), Kate O'Brien refers to '... a harmony of feeling and conclusion which can only be accidental, but is all the more persuasive for that.' This harmony consists of such elements as common sense, dislike of complication, a strong preference for the concrete over the abstract, a certain quietness of mind, a shrewd, tolerant judgement, a greater interest in character and action than in ideas. These statements are often qualified by their authors with portraits of some non-conforming genius, but there remains an anchor holding the British genius to its bed-rock of awareness of, and sympathy with, routine and the common day. In addition to sharing these basic characteristics, the authors also showed confidence in things British and in the expression of certain traditional values that were taken for granted. Although written for the most part at a time of great danger, 93 of the volumes being published between 1941 and 1945, there was complete certainty that Britain would survive.

The impact of the war on Britain's future wealth and place in the world was obviously not a factor that needed to be taken into account when describing what had already been achieved. This does not mean that the authors were complacent or backward looking; their brief was to describe British society as it was and had been, not how it might become, but they were sensitive towards and concerned about modern developments. The voices that can be heard from all the volumes are those of assured, educated and confident people, sometimes sceptical and even cynical, but never doubting that there was something very worthwhile to protect in British institutions, attitudes and achievements and keen to promote them to a wider public in Britain and abroad. Nicholas Garland, the cartoonist, writing about wartime propaganda posters in June 1994 in the *Daily Telegraph* during the fiftieth anniversary of the D-Day landings, referred to '... a whiff of wartime and post-war Britain. It is intelligent, sensible, quiet and ironic.' This is the flavour also of BIP.

In some ways the series provides the obverse of the gloomy picture that one can get from reading the political polemics of the 'thirties; it rises above the temporary difficulties of the depression and the war, and avoids the temptation of ideological debate, displaying instead the more enduring riches and qualities of what had been achieved by British people. This straightforward pride in British characteristics, an uncomplicated love of Britain and things British, and an urge to educate and explain, are among its most attractive features. There was no nostalgia, no yearning for a world that was gone, but rather a recognition of the importance of individual genius and of a thousand worthwhile values and characteristics which would always remain worth keeping. The BIP series was, and still is, a ready made national curriculum that provides any literate Britisher with a reasonably complete picture of their country, its people and their achievements. In some small ways it might be a little out of date. Writing in 1983 in a reprint of some of the volumes on literature[1], Lord David Cecil confessed that some of his judgements in 1941 had been immature and that he had in particular devoted far too little space to Gerard Manley Hopkins and Edward Thomas '... both of whom I have come to regard as among the greatest English writers of the last hundred years.' Other authors too might regret some of the judgements they made during those war years. More important than such second thoughts, however, is how much of the original thought remains immensely worthwhile. Events since the 1939-45 war have not made the series and its values out of date: subsequent events can never reduce the value of what was achieved in the thousands of years that preceded them, and which were recorded so well in the superbly written and beautifully illustrated essays that make up 'Britain In Pictures'.

[1] *Impressions of English Literature* pub 1984 Thames and Hudson, see 134 in chronological list.

PART 2: THE BOOKS

W.J. Turner
(photograph by Howard Coster reproduced by courtesy of the National Portrait Gallery, London)

Some of the 'British People In Pictures' volumes

The 'British Commonwealth In Pictures' series

Introduction

Part 2 consists of three lists relating to the individual volumes. First a chronological list of all the books with information about the various editions and brief biographical details of authors. This is followed by an alphabetical list of authors giving a cross reference to the chronological list. There is then a subject list showing how individual volumes fit into the broad subject categories and which again refers to the volume number in the chronological list. These are followed by an index which relates to Parts 1 and 2 and includes the titles of the books with a cross reference to the volume number, and people and events from Part 1 with the page reference. Thus the reader or collector using the lists and the index should be able to trace details of a book provided that the title or the number or the broad subject or the author is known.

For readers and collectors, BIP provides many delights, not the least being that individual volumes are modestly priced. Condition, of course, affects price, but most volumes can still be bought for £2 — £4 in reasonable condition, including the dust-jacket; I saw several volumes in a bookshop in Cecil Court, Central London in 1993 at these sorts of prices. Outside London, oddly, prices are often higher; in the same year, a very large selection in Llangollen, North Wales, was priced in a range from £7.50 to £10 each. Some volumes command much higher prices; one collector refused to buy *British Farm Stock* (132) at £29 in 1993, so priced because it was said to be scarce, a reasonable comment as only 5,780 copies were printed. (See sales figures pp 120-123) George Orwell's *The English People* (100) seems usually to be the most expensive, almost never less than £20 and often more. Any by authors whose other books are widely collected, such as the volume by Graham Greene, are also highly priced. Many volumes are offered for sale in bad condition; the spines are easily broken and the paper does seem to be especially susceptible to foxing; the higher prices would be for copies in good condition. Paul Breman, a London bookseller, advertised in June 1994 a complete set of 126 volumes at £385 which included the quite scarce six volumes of 'The English Poets In Pictures'.

All the books are worth reading and all of them are beautiful to look at, so it is worthwhile seeking to build up a complete collection, but what does complete mean? Peter Eads in his *Private Library* article, autumn 1986, refers to significant differences between editions of *English Pottery and China* (77). Other volumes too were revised between prints to make corrections or to change illustrations. Any differences I have seen, or which have been noted and recorded by others, are included in the appropriate entry of the chronological list. As I have not seen, or become aware of, all the different reprints I have not been able to make a comprehensive comparison. More important than minor differences between different reprints are completely different editions, for example the rare cloth-covered editions and the various translations.

Individual collectors will make their own decisions on how complete they want their collection to be. Leaving aside variations in printings and different editions and impressions, a basic collection would consist of 113 volumes of 'The British People In Pictures', seven volumes of 'The British Commonwealth In Pictures' and six volumes of 'The English Poets In Pictures', making a total of 126 in all. Then there are the seven omnibus volumes which are worth having because they are so handsome. For those readers and collectors who are interested mainly in obtaining this basic collection, the chronological list will be more than adequate.

DETAILS COMMON TO ALL THE BOOKS

Some details, such as those about publisher and printers, are common to all or most of the books and are set out below so as to avoid needless repetition in each entry of the chronological list. When a book does not conform to the common pattern, this is pointed out in its individual entry.

The Series

There were three series — Series 1 'The British People In Pictures', Series 2 'The British Commonwealth In Pictures', and Series 3 'The English Poets In Pictures', which together made up 'Britain In Pictures'. That this arrangement was intended from the start is clear from the first headed notepaper used when the editorial group originally worked from Penns in the Rocks. However, despite this early use of three titles and a generic title, when the first 16 volumes were published, the title 'Britain In Pictures' was used as the title for Series 1 and there was no general title for the three series. It was only from Volume 17, *English Education*, that 'Britain In Pictures' began to be shown on the books themselves as the generic title, with the other three titles being used for the specific series. This development is clear from the reverse and inside reverse of the dust-jackets and from the half-title page. Accordingly I have used the title 'Britain In Pictures' to denote all three series and used the specific titles to indicate the separate series. (A fourth series, 'The Nations And Britain' was started soon afterwards, but it is quite separate and was never part of BIP.)

Publisher

The three series were published by William Collins of London. The first ten volumes recorded on the title page that they were:

Published for
PENNS IN THE ROCKS PRESS
by
WILLIAM COLLINS OF LONDON

'Penns in the Rocks' was the name of Dorothy Wellesley's house in Withyham, near Groombridge, Sussex, and she used the imprint for her own books. After volume ten that imprint was no longer used for BIP and the publication of later volumes was styled either as by:

WILLIAM COLLINS OF LONDON

or by:

COLLINS . 14 ST. JAMES'S PLACE . LONDON

These variations do not seem worth recording for each volume as the publisher throughout was Collins. On the title page of all volumes is a publisher's device. In all but three of the volumes this device is a drawing of a temple, based on the Temple to the poet Yeats which Dorothy Wellesley had had built in the grounds of Penns in the Rocks. The three exceptions are *British Butterflies* (125), *Children's Illustrated Books* (126), and *British Farm Stock* (132), each of which contain the Collins' device of a fountain. This change must have had some connection with the death of Walter Turner, but other volumes published at the same time retained the temple device; it remains a puzzle. (See also note on Special Editions p 73 which explains about two variations in the publisher's imprint used for the rare, cloth bound volumes.)

Producer

All the books in all three series were produced by Adprint Limited London. (See Part 1 pp 25-27 for details of Adprint.)

Printers

All the Omnibus series and most, a total of 53, of the individual volumes were printed by Clarke and Sherwell Ltd of Northampton. Smaller numbers were printed by William Collins Sons Ltd., Glasgow, (a total of 23); Jarrold and Sons Ltd, Norwich, (10); Sun Engraving Co Ltd., London and Watford, (10); William Brown and Co Ltd., London, (7); and 8 by an unidentified printer somewhere in Great Britain. The firm of W.S. Cowell, Ltd., Ipswich, printed one! I have not recorded the details in each entry because the printing was always in accordance with the standard specification; there being no scope for variation of type-setting or format, there seemed little point repeating the various printers' names in the entries. There were some differences in the type of paper used in different volumes, for example colour illustrations in a few volumes were reproduced on paper with a matt surface instead of the shiny art paper used for most volumes, but usually all production aspects were the same.

General Description of Books

Peter Eads in his *Private Library* article of autumn 1986 refers to the contract of 6 May 1940 between William Collins, the publisher, and Adprint, the producer. This agreed on the specifications of the volumes and other matters. He sent me his copy of a second and more extensive agreement reached on 7 June 1941, that copy being signed by W.A.R. Collins. The general specification of the books agreed was:

> (a) *'Britain in Pictures'* trimmed size 8¾" × 6⅜" (untrimmed 9" × 6½") 8-12 colour plates in 6 colour offset or in 4 colour deep etched half-tone letterpress, and 48 pages in monochrome offset or one colour photogravure containing approximately 12-30 monochrome pictures in the text.
> Paper Double Crown 50lbs woodfree offset.
> Binding and Printing of Cover similar to titles already produced.
>
> (b) *'The British Commonwealth in Pictures'*
> Exactly as 'Britain in Pictures'.
>
> (c) *'The English Poets in Pictures'* trimmed size 7" × 4⅜" (untrimmed 7¼" × 4½") 4 colour plates in 6 colour offset or in 4 colour deep etched half-tone letterpress and 80 pages in monochrome offset containing approximately 12-25 illustrations and plates together as facsimile reproductions of old manuscript pages or old book pages of first editions. Several of the text pages to contain facsimile reproductions of Vignettes

The Books 69

    small drawings ornaments and other similar matters in relation to the production of old books of first or other famous old editions.
    Paper Double Crown 50lbs woodfree offset.
    Binding and printing of cover as in (a).

    The Poets are so different in size and appearance from the other two series that they can easily be overlooked in bookshops. The dust-jacket and cover of each volume replicate one another exactly in colour and design. All six volumes had the same cover and jacket design of a lyre within a wreath of laurel leaves, the only difference between volumes being the colour of the jacket and cover.

    The dust-jackets and the covers of the People and Commonwealth series also replicate one another exactly, but the colours and design are more striking than the Poets; and those of the People series are simpler than the Commonwealth series, usually being in pale pastel shades with the title in large white capitals at the top and the author's name in capitals at the bottom. In between was a stylised design related to the subject of the volume, except in three cases (*British Cartoonists, Caricaturists and Comic Artists* (25), *British Romantic Artists* (34), and *British Drawings* (105) where reproductions of prints were used.) The whole effect was striking and unfussy, giving them a very modern look. The jackets and covers of the Commonwealth volumes used repetitive motifs appropriate to the country being described.

Number of Pages

Usually in the People and Commonwealth series there were 48 pages, except for seven volumes in 1948/49 (numbers 122, 123, 124, 126, 127, 131 and 132) which had 50 pages. The six in the Poets series each had 80 pages. Colour plates were additional to the numbered pages.

Editorial Committee

The first six volumes, which are part of the People and Commonwealth series, contain the names of the original Editorial Committee (Dorothy Wellesley, Hilda Matheson and W.J. Turner) on the advertisement page facing the title page. Volumes seven and eight, which are part of the Poets series, like all six volumes in that series, omit any reference to editors other than Dorothy Wellesley. In volumes nine and ten Hilda Matheson's name has been replaced by that of Lord David Cecil. In the volumes which follow, except for those in the Poets series, only the name of the General Editor, W.J. Turner, appears. That is until volumes 122-126, and 129-130 when there is no reference to the editor. Then in volumes 127-128 and 131-132 Turner's name appears once again!

These changes were made following first, the death of Hilda Matheson in 1941 and secondly, the death of Walter Turner in 1946.

CONVENTIONS USED IN THE CHRONOLOGICAL LIST

The chronological list is the main source of information about each book, its various editions and author. Each entry contains the volume number, title, author, series in the case of the Poets and the Commonwealth, subject area, number of pages when different from 48, number of illustrations, date of first publication, dates of reviews in *The Times Literary Supplement* and *The Observer*, reprints of the standard editions, details of non-standard editions, any special features of the volume, sales figures, and biographical details of the author. The notes which follow provide information on the criteria and conventions used for each of these components of an entry.

Volume Number

The volume number is that allocated by the publisher and appears at the top and bottom of the spine of the dust-jacket, but not on the cover. Numbers began to be used in 1945, the first to be numbered being C.E. Vulliamy's *English Letter Writers* (81). The use of volume numbers results mainly, but not entirely, in a list in date order. Because of the way in which numbers were introduced late in the series, consecutive numbers do not always mean consecutive publication. Books published before numbers were introduced were numbered subsequently, when reprinted, or a number was simply allocated in a list held by the publisher, and chronology was not strictly observed; and later volumes were given numbers in anticipation of publication dates which were not, in the event, always realised. Nevertheless, despite the uncertainties, book number order has been retained because it helps with identification and facilitates cross reference.

Title and Author

These are shown as they appear on the title page. Variations between editions, or even in the same edition between the title page, the dust-jacket, the cover and other pages, are referred to in the entry. The author's name as shown on the title page and the dust-jacket was usually a short version of their full name, and the full version is given later in the entry. The surname of Ralph Burdon, Ngaio

The Books 71

Marsh's co-author for *New Zealand* (26) was spelled incorrectly as Burden and this has been retained in the heading, but corrected later in the entry. For volumes written by two authors the order of names follows that on the title page, although in some cases this is different from the order on the dust-jacket and cover.

Series

Most of the volumes are in 'The British People In Pictures' series and for these the series is not noted; I have used the initials BC for the seven published in 'The British Commonwealth In Pictures' series and EP for the six in 'The English Poets In Pictures' series.

Subject Area

This is the sub-division, such as 'Art and Craftsmanship', within which each volume was advertised on dust-jackets. There are nine of these sub-divisions and the volumes in each are shown in full in the subject list at pp 128-131.

Number of Pages

As most volumes had 48 pages, the number of pages is shown only for those with a different number.

Illustrations

These are the number of illustrations in the first, standard edition, with attention drawn to any discrepancies between the list of illustrations printed after the title page and those which actually appear in the body of the text. The number of colour plates was usually either 8 or 12, but in the Poets series and also volumes 126, 127, 131 and 132 of the People series there were only four. The number of black-and-white illustrations varied greatly. In most entries these are recorded in total without distinguishing between types of illustration, except that where the volume lists vignettes and tailpieces separately they are recorded as such in the entry. When illustrations are photographs, rather than reproductions of drawings or paintings, this is recorded. There were sometimes changes in illustration between the first and any revised edition and I have indicated these when I have seen the differences for myself or they have been noted in a published article or list. As I have not seen every impression or revision of a volume, I am sure that there are omissions in some of the entries.

Publication Date

The first date shown in an entry is the year of first publication shown on the title page of each volume. For many of the books it is not possible to be more precise about publication date than the year of publication or reprint. The month of publication was not recorded in the books and the publisher's records have been destroyed. In some cases a little more precision is possible, for example by making use of information on dust-jackets, but, as references in one volume to the date of publication of another are sometimes incorrect, these are not always a sound source. Bibliographies sometimes provide an exact date, but for most BIP authors there are no bibliographies. The British Library Catalogue does not help as it has introduced a new number series which bears no relation to the publisher's series. (Indeed, this catalogue is odd in other respects in the way in which it deals with BIP. For example, the whole series is recorded under the name of Dorothy Wellesley rather than W.J. Turner.) To add further complication, sometimes the volume number places a book in sequence with volumes of another year. The books were often actually published much later than the date shown on the title page. For example, Charles Hadfield's volume, *English Rivers and Canals* (84), records on the title page a publication date of 1945, when in fact, as already recorded in the text (page 35), it was published in March 1946; *British Soldiers* (58) and *The English at Table* (51) were both published in 1944 according to their title pages, but they were reviewed in March 1945, and their volume numbers place them within books published in 1943. There are so many other examples that it would be tedious to list them here, but the discrepancy is noted in each case in the entry. This is the reason why books are not listed in order of publication date and also why dates of reviews are shown (see below).

Reviews

These are the dates of reviews which appeared in *The Observer* (O) newspaper and *The Times Literary Supplement* (TLS). These have been included in order to help to establish more precisely the actual publication dates. I believe the entries to be a complete record of those reviews because I have referred to all the issues published in the years 1941 to 1951. Sometimes a review was recorded in the TLS index, but could not be found in the issue referred to. My reason for selecting these two publications is that a quick survey of other newspapers and periodicals for 1941 indicated that I was most likely to find reviews in the O and the TLS.

The Books

Reprints, Revisions, New Editions and Non-Standard Editions

In each entry the review date is followed by dates of reprints of the standard edition, that is the English edition with thin papered board covers and matching dust-jacket. After the first edition, which is recognised by the date on the title page, I have used the word *impression* to describe subsequent issues with the date which was recorded, usually, on the verso of the title page, but sometimes on the title page itself! These impressions are listed so far as I know them; by that I mean that I have listed either ones that I have seen, or which I know have been seen and listed by other people. Mr Joseph S. F. Murdoch of Pennsylvania, Mr Paul Breman of London, Mr D. E. Wickham of Kent and Mr Michael Sedgely of Sussex all sent me their own lists of the various editions they had collected and I have used them as authoritative records of volumes I have not seen.

The Private Library articles already referred to (pp 8 and 68) record several non-standard editions. These were bound in cloth, the colour of which varied, and had gilt or other coloured decorations and lettering. Some have been found with dust-jackets in the same style as the standard edition. The examples seen and recorded by collectors to date were "Published for / Penns In The Rocks Press / By / William Collins of London"; or by "Britain In Pictures Limited"; or by "Britain In Pictures Publishers / Bahamas". There are also some translations, usually in the same style as the standard volumes and published by Collins, but there is at least one in French which was published by Éditions Du Chêne, Paris, not Collins; details are given in the appropriate entry. I have not been able to find out much about these non-standard editions except, as recorded in Part 1 p 29, that Adprint established an office in Nassau, which was in the sterling area, as a means of getting into the USA market. The Nassau office was established in 1941, followed by the setting up of a fully owned subsidiary of Adprint in New York, the Chanticleer Press, which looked after the Nassau operation and sales in the USA. Use was also made of Crown publishers in America. This development explains to some extent the 'Bahamas' editions, but not why some were produced in cloth with gilt decoration.

Finally, some of the standard editions were reprinted in 1987 by Bracken Books. Those I have seen were without dust-jackets and had a hard, glossy cover. The contents had been rearranged in order to bring the colour plates into two groups of four, but otherwise they seemed to be identical to the standard edition. These reprints are listed in the appropriate entry. The publisher refused to tell me how many they had reprinted, but *British Photographers* (71), *English Pottery and China* (77), *Sporting Pictures of England* (87), *English Watercolour*

Painters (88), *Early Britain* (92), *British Clocks and Clockmakers (111)* and *Roman Britain* (113) have been seen.

Sales Figures

Each entry, except for volumes in the Poets series, omnibus volumes and *Australia* (5), records the total books published in the edition (that is, the standard edition including all reprints) (E); total sales up to 31 December 1951 (S); total unsold as at 31 December 1951 (U); and sales, usually remaindered sales, in 1952 (R). At the end of the Chronological List (pp 120-123) there is a Schedule of Sales arranged in descending order. As explained in the notes preceding the Schedule, the figures for the years up to and including 1951 are taken from photocopies of manuscript schedules prepared by Kenneth Helmore, Adprint's Company Secretary, and sent to me by Joyce Howell. The notes comment on the accuracy of the figures and explain the origin of the figures for 1952.

Biographical Details

The information always includes, when known, date of birth and death, education, and a career summary, which is very brief for well-known authors. More information is given, when available, for authors who are less well known and who are not in standard reference books; sometimes more information is given even for well-known authors when it is of particular interest. There are still four authors about whom I have found almost nothing. The standard references consulted were *Who's Who* and *Who Was Who* (WW), *The Dictionary of National Biography* (DNB), *Contemporary Authors* (CA), and obituaries, mainly from *The Times*. Use was also made of biographies, autobiographies and diaries. Many people helped with information about authors not included in reference books and I regret that space does not permit me to acknowledge them all by name.

Omnibus Volumes

The seven omnibus volumes, which were not numbered by the publisher, are shown at the end of the numbered sequence in the chronological list. I have given each of them a number to facilitate cross reference.

Volumes Advertised But Not Published

Books planned and advertised, but not published, are included.

CHRONOLOGICAL LIST

KEY TO ABBREVIATIONS

The abbreviations below are shown in the order in which they appear in the entries. No key is thought necessary for abbreviations for Queen's Honours, degrees and other such well known initials.

BC = 'The British Commonwealth In Pictures' EP = 'The English Poets In Pictures' pp = pages cp = colour plates sp = sepia plates bw = black-and-white illustrations v = vignette t = tail-piece ph = photographs

Pub = published O = *The Observer* newspaper TLS = *The Times Literary Supplement* imp = impression

OV = Omnibus Volume FOB = Festival of Britain 1951

E = total edition S = total sales to end 1951 U = total left unsold at end 1951 R = remaindered sales in 1952

b = born d = died ed = educated BP = 'The British People In Pictures' BIP = 'Britain In Pictures'.

Initials at the end of an entry are to the three standard biographical sources which contain details of the author, namely WW = *Who's Who* (and *Who Was Who* for dead authors) DNB = *Dictionary of National Biography* and CA = *Contemporary Authors*. These are recorded to help readers searching for more information and do not signify that the sources have necessarily been drawn on for the information in the entry.

1 The English Poets. Lord David Cecil
Literature and Belles Lettres. 8 cp, 13 bw.
Pub March 1941. O 23 March, TLS 5 April. 2nd imp 1942, 3rd 1945, 5th 1947. Reprinted for FOB.
Included in OV *Impressions of British Literature* (134).
Maroon paper board edition, no dust-jacket, gold lettering on spine and gold decoration on cover with laurel wreath device in centre, pub 1941, for Penns in the Rocks Press by William Collins of London. Also a blue cloth edition, no date, white lettering, dust-jacket identical to that of the standard edition, pub Britain In Pictures Limited; and an undated edition pub Britain in Pictures Publishers, Bahamas.
E 66,371, S 60,247, U 6,024.

Lord Edward Christian David Gascoyne Cecil CH, university teacher and literary critic, b 9 April 1902, d 1 January 1986, younger son of the fourth Marquis of Salisbury, ed Eton and Christ Church College Oxford. Fellow of Wadham then New College Oxford, Goldsmiths' Professor of English Literature, Oxford, 1948-69. Enjoyed a brief period of celebrity as a member of TV's Brains Trust, but his main claim to fame is his literary criticism in such books as *The Stricken Deer* 1929. See Part 1 p61 for his second thoughts about his BP volume. WW CA

2 British Sport. Eric Parker
Country Life and Sport. 12 cp, 18 bw (not 17 as stated on tp) including 8 ph.
Pub March 1941. O 23 March, TLS 5 April.
Brown cloth edition, no date, trophy decoration and lettering in gold, pub Britain In Pictures Limited.
E 16,460, S 13,998, U 2,462.

Eric Frederick Moore Searle Parker, editor, author and journalist, b 8 October 1870, d 13 February 1955, ed Eton and Merton College Oxford. Schoolmaster, then from 1900 to 1937 edited successively *St. James' Gazette*, *Country Gentleman*, *Land and Water*, *Gamekeeper*, and *The Field*. Prolific author of country books. WW DNB

3 English Music. W.J. Turner
Art and Craftsmanship. 12 cp, 21 bw.
Pub March 1941. O 23 March, TLS 5 April. 2nd imp 1942, 3rd 1943, 4th (revised) 1947.
Orange cloth edition, no date, gilt lettering, pub Britain In Pictures Limited.
E 61,036, S 52,893, U 8,143. R 1,223. See also entries 80 and 133-139.

Walter James Redfern Turner, poet, author, music and theatre critic, journalist, playwright, b 13 October 1889, d 18 November 1946, ed Scotch College and School of Mines Melbourne. A prolific writer who in addition to his poetry, autobiographical and fictional works, wrote biographies of Beethoven, Berlioz, Mozart and Wagner. (See also Part 1 pp 22-23 and 39-41 for other biographical details.) WW DNB

4 The Government of Britain. G.M. Young
History and Achievement. 12 cp, 16 bw.
Pub March 1941. O 23 March, TLS 5 April. 2nd imp 1942.
Brown cloth edition, no date, gilt lettering, pub Britain In Pictures Limited.
E 26,393, S 25,682, U 711.

George Malcolm Young CB, civil servant, scholar, historian, b 29 April 1882, d 18 November 1959, ed St Paul's School and Balliol College Oxford. Secretary to Board of Education 1911, Cabinet Office 1916, Joint-Secretary of Ministry of Reconstruction 1917, but abandoned public service after war and devoted himself to writing. His books include the magnificent extended essay *Victorian England: Portrait of an Age* 1936. WW DNB CA

5 Australia. Arnold Haskell
BC, 12 cp, 23 bw.
Pub March 1941. O 23 March, TLS 5 April.
Included in OV *The British Commonwealth and Empire* (133).
South American edition in Spanish, no date, red cloth with black kangaroo decoration and dust-jacket identical to the standard edition.
E, S, U — no figures.

Arnold Lionel Haskell CBE, writer, lecturer, ballet director, b 19 July 1903, d 15 November 1980, ed Westminster School and Trinity College Cambridge. Reader in Heinemann's 1927-32, visited USA with Russian Ballet 1933-34, dance critic of *The Daily*

Telegraph 1935-38, Director of the Royal Ballet School 1946-1965. He was a great educator and populariser of ballet, writing more than 20 books on the subject, including *Balletomania* 1934. His other books on Australia were *Waltzing Matilda: a Background to Australia* 1940, and *The Australians* 1948. WW DNB CA

6 East Africa. Elspeth Huxley
BC, 12 cp, 17 bw.
Pub March 1941. O 23 March, TLS 5 April.
Included in OV *The British Commonwealth and Empire* (133).
E 14,273, S 13,474, U 899.

Elspeth Josceline Huxley CBE, (Mrs Gervas Huxley), author, b 23 July 1907, ed European School Nairobi, Universities of Reading (UK) and Cornell (USA). Assistant Press Officer to Empire Marketing Board 1929-32, then travel and writing. Her many books include novels, history, in particular of East Africa, and books linking history, politics and agriculture. Member of the Monkton Advisory Commission on Central Africa 1959. WW CA

7 Shelley. Dorothy Wellesley (Editor)
EP, 80 pp, 4 cp, 12 bw.
Pub March 1941. O 23 March, TLS 5 April.
E, S, U — no figures. See also entries 8, 19, 20, 43 and 44.

Dorothy Violet Wellesley, Duchess of Wellington, poet, b 30 July 1889, d 11 July 1956. In 1914 she married Lord Gerald Wellesley who succeeded his nephew as seventh Duke of Wellington in 1943. As well as editing EP, she was editor of the Hogarth Living Poets series and published several books of her own poetry, one of them, *Selections from the Poems of Dorothy Wellesley*, with an introduction by Yeats. (See also Part 1 pp 21-22 and 32 for other biographical details.) DNB

8 Byron. Dorothy Wellesley (Editor)
EP, 80 pp, 4 cp, 20 bw.
Pub March 1941. O 23 March, TLS 5 April.
E, S, U — no figures. See also entries 7, 19, 20, 43 and 44.

9 Canada. Lady Tweedsmuir
BC, 12 cp, 32 bw including 13 ph.
Pub 1941, TLS 5 July. 2nd imp 1943.
Included in OV *The British Commonwealth and Empire* (133).
Green cloth edition, 1941, red maple leaf decoration and dust-jacket identical to standard edition.
E 13,601 (sic), S 24,162, U oversold.

Susan, Lady Tweedsmuir, writer, b 1883, d 21 March 1977, ed at home. Author of a study of Wellington, *The Sword of State*, and several children's books. Her knowledge of Canada was based on her four and a half years residence as wife of the Governor-General, the author John Buchan, whom she married in 1907. WW

10 India. Sir Firozkhan Noon
BC, 12 cp, 26 bw including 17 ph.
Pub 1941. TLS 5 July.
Included in OV *The British Commonwealth and Empire* (133).
E 14,398, S 13,770, U 628, R 2.

(Sir) Firozkhan Noon, diplomat and politician, b 7 May 1893, d 9 December 1970, ed Chiefs' College Lahore, Oxford, and Inner Temple. High Commissioner for India 1937, but gave up that office, together with his knighthood, when he joined Mr Jinnah's party to promote the establishment of an independent Pakistan. Prime Minister of Pakistan 1957. WW

11 English Villages. Edmund Blunden
Country Life and Sport. 12 cp, 24 bw including 5 tp.
Pub 1941. TLS 6 September. 2nd imp 1942, 4th 1945, 5th 1947.
Included in OV *The Englishman's Country* (135).
E 62,440, S 56,883, U 5,557, R 104.

Edmund Charles Blunden CBE MC, poet, teacher, critic, b 1 November 1896, d 20 January 1974, ed Christ's Hospital School and Queen's College Oxford. Served in France and Belgium 1914-18 with Royal Sussex Regiment, awarded MC 1916. Professor of English Literature Tokyo 1924-27, Fellow and Tutor Merton College Oxford 1931-43, UK Liaison Mission to Tokyo 1947-50, Professor of English University of Hong Kong 1953-64, Professor of Poetry University of Oxford 1966-68. Hawthornden Prize 1922. Queen's Medal for Poetry 1956. Author of many books of poetry and literary criticism. WW DNB CA

12 British Medicine. R. McNair Wilson
Science, Medicine and Engineering. 8 cp, 20 bw.
Pub 1941. TLS 6 September.
Black cloth edition, no date, gilt lettering, pub Britain In Pictures Limited.
E 16,175, S 13,961, U 2,214.

Dr Robert McNair Wilson, medical doctor and writer, b 22 May 1882, d 29 November 1963, ed Glasgow Academy and University of Glasgow. In addition to medical practice, he was medical correspondent of *The Times* 1914-42, editor of Oxford Medical Publications, Consultant Physician to the Ministry of Pensions, and a prolific author of medical books, biographies, and works on or related to Napoleon and the French Revolution. He also stood, unsuccessfully, as a Liberal candidate in Saffron Walden. WW

13 British Statesmen. Ernest Barker
History and Achievement. 12 cp, 17 bw.
Pub 1941. TLS 6 September. 2nd imp 1942
Green cloth edition, no date, gilt lettering; also, in buff cloth, a 2nd ed, no date, blue lettering; both pub Britain In Pictures Limited.
E 22,422, S 20,223, U 2,199.

Professor Sir Ernest Barker, historian, b 23 September 1874, d 17 February 1960, ed

Manchester Grammar School and Balliol College Oxford. Lecturer at Merton 1898-1905, Wadham 1899-1909, St John's 1909-13, and New College 1913-20 all Oxford colleges. Principal King's College London 1920-27, Professor of Political Science Cambridge 1929-39, and Cologne 1947-48. Son of a miner and scholarship boy who never lost sight of his roots and was a lifelong friend of the Co-operative movement, the Workers' Educational Association and The National Council for Social Service. WW DNB CA

14 British Scientists. Sir Richard Gregory
Science and Engineering. 12 cp, 19 bw.
Pub 1941. No review in O or TLS.
Red cloth edition, no date, gilt lettering, also an edition in rust boards, dated 1941, both pub Britain In Pictures Limited; and another, undated, pub Britain In Pictures Publishers, Bahamas.
E 17,702, S 15,711, U 1,991, R 153.

Sir Richard Arman Gregory, scientist and journalist, b 29 January 1864 d 15 September 1952, ed Wesleyan day school, Queen Elizabeth's Hospital school and, finally, elementary school before leaving at age 12 to earn his living as a clicker in a shoe factory. After evening classes he became a laboratory assistant, then a student-teacher until in 1887 he took a first class degree in astronomy and physics. He shared some of his student days with H.G. Wells who became a life-long friend. His articles on astronomy began to appear in *Nature* and he became a freelance lecturer and writer. In 1893 he became Assistant editor of *Nature* and was editor from 1919 to 1938. Under him it became an international journal and the accepted channel of communication in the scientific world. From 1898 until 1917 he was Professor of Astronomy at Queen's College, London, but his main contribution to science was as a populariser, the '... greatest scientific journalist of his day', and as a scientific policy maker, drawing attention to the link between science, government and national welfare. WW DNB

15 English Country Houses. V. Sackville-West
Country Life and Sport. 8 cp, 23 bw.
Pub 1941. TLS 1 November. 2nd imp 1942, 3rd 1943, 4th 1945, 5th 1947. Reprinted for FOB.
Included in OV *The Englishman's Country* (135).
Green cloth edition, no date, gilt lettering, pub Britain In Pictures Limited; also a French translation, green paperboard, pub 1947 by Éditions Du Chêne, Paris.
E 46,158, S 51,606, U oversold, R 5320.

The Hon Victoria Mary Sackville-West, writer and gardener, b 9 March 1892, d 2 June 1962, ed at home, which was Knole in Sevenoaks, one of the greatest country houses in England. Wrote many books of poetry, novels, history, and about the countryside and gardens; by the age of 18 she had written eight novels, one of them in French, and five plays. Her poem *The Land* won the Hawthornden Prize in 1927, her novel *The Garden* won the Heinemann Prize in 1947 and her book *The Edwardians* published in 1930 was a best seller. From 1946-61 she wrote a gardening column for *The Observer*; and with her husband (Sir) Harold Nicolson created the garden at Sissinghurst, Kent, now owned by The National Trust. She was a great friend of Dorothy Wellesley and Hilda Matheson and wrote the latter's obituary for *The Spectator* and the DNB article on Dorothy Wellesley. Her own biography, *Vita*, was written by Victoria Glendinning, pub Weidenfeld and Nicolson 1983. WW DNB CA

16 English Farming. Sir John Russell
Country Life and Sport. 12 cp, 11 bw, 3 tp, 4 graphs.
Pub 1941. No review in O or TLS. 2nd imp 1942, 3rd 1943, 4th 1946. Introduction by Henry Williamson, author of *Tarka the Otter* and other stories of the countryside. Green cloth edition, no date, gilt lettering, pub Britain In Pictures Limited; also a Turkish translation, no date, paperboard covers, pub Collins London.
E 41,108, S 39,848, U 1,260, R 89.

Sir Edward John Russell OBE, agriculturalist, b 31 October 1872, d 12 July 1965, ed University College of Wales Aberystwyth and Victoria University Manchester. Lecturer in chemistry at Manchester 1898-1901, Head of Chemical Department at Wye College, Kent 1901-07, Chemist at Rothamsted Research Station 1907-12 becoming Director 1912-43. He was Director of the Imperial Bureau of Soil Science 1928-43. In addition to his soil science publications he wrote generally on agriculture and science, and an autobiography *The Land Called Me* 1956. He was always fighting for more money for research and is said to have shown skill amounting to genius in getting money from private sources, including sufficient to buy the Rothamsted estate when the public trustee was proposing to sell it for development. WW CA

17 English Education. Kenneth Lindsay
Education and Religion. 8 cp, 18 bw including 7 ph.
Pub 1941. O 18, TLS 24 January 1942.
E 17,079, S 18,898, U oversold.

Kenneth Martin Lindsay MP, educationist and administrator, b 16 September 1897, d 4 March 1991, ed St Olave's School and Worcester College Oxford. Research Fellow Toynbee Hall 1923-26, Secretary Political and Economic Planning 1931-35, Parliamentary Secretary to the Board of Education 1937-40, Member of Parliament for Kilmarnock Boroughs 1933-45, and for the Combined English Universities 1945-50. As well as being a founder of the Youth Service he was also involved in establishing CEMA, the predecessor to The Arts Council. WW CA

18 South Africa. Sarah Gertrude Millin
BC, 12 cp, 28 bw including 10 ph and 4 tp.
Pub 1941. TLS 17 January 1942.
Included in OV *The British Commonwealth and Empire* (133).
E 16,770, S 15,736, U 1034.

Sarah Gertrude Millin, writer, b 1889, d 6 July 1968, ed Girls' High School Kimberley. *The Times*' obituarist referred to her '... clear, clenched, prose, with never a word wasted ... a vision which was incisive and astringent ...' and to her 'spare and taut style.' Her other books about South Africa include a definitive history, *The South Africans*, 1926, later published in a revised edition as *The People of South Africa*, and Biographies of Cecil Rhodes 1933 and Smuts 1936. Her autobiography, *The Night is*

Long, was published in 1939 and her diaries *The Reeling Earth* in 1945. She wrote 16 novels, her first popular success being *God's Stepchildren* in 1924. She also wrote three books of short stories. Both the content and style of her BC volume should have made it one of the best-sellers, but it wasn't. For further information on this remarkable writer see Jacobus P. L. Snyman's *The Works of Sarah Gertrude Millin* 1955 and Morage Whyte's *Bibliography* of 1952. WW CA

19 Tennyson. Dorothy Wellesley (Editor)
EP, 80 p, 4 cp, 22 bw.
Pub 1941. No review in O or TLS.
Undated ed pub Britain In Pictures Limited.
E, S, U, no figures. See also entries 7, 8, 20, 43 and 44.

20 Keats. Dorothy Wellesley (Editor)
EP, 80 p, 4 cp, 18 bw.
Pub 1941. No review in O or TLS.
E, S, U, no figures. See also entries 7, 8, 19, 43 and 44.

21 The Story of Scotland. F. Fraser Darling
Topographical History. 8 cp, 19 bw including 2 tp.
Pub 1942. O 29 March and 19 April, TLS 2 May. 2nd imp 1942, 4th 1947.
E 57,647, S 51,105, U 6542, R 139. See also entry 52.

Dr (Sir) Frank Fraser Darling, scientist and author, b 23 June 1903, d 22 October 1979, ed University of Edinburgh. After initial work on animal genetics, he worked and lived from 1933-53 in the wildest parts of Scotland, supported by Leverhulme, Carnegie and similar grants. At the time he wrote this BP volume, he was still treated with suspicion by the scientific establishment, being regarded as too much of a populariser. It was not until the 'fifties, first in Edinburgh and then in the USA, that he began to obtain approval for his work on ecology and wildlife conservation. From 1959-72 he was Vice-President of the Conservation Foundation in Washington DC. In 1969 he gave the BBC Reith Lectures on the subject of *Wilderness and Plenty* and from 1970-73 he was a member of the Royal Commission on Environmental Pollution. WW DNB CA.

22 British Mountaineers. F.S. Smythe
History and Achievement. 8 cp, 24 bw including 4 tp.
Pub 1942. TLS 21 February. There are mistakes in the first edition; on page eight, the sixteenth century should read eighteenth, on pages 15 and 16 the captions on the portraits have been transposed, and on page 17 the reference to the Walker 'brothers' should be to father and son. 2nd imp 1946.
Included in OV *British Adventure* (137).
Buff cloth edition, no date, turquoise lettering, pub Britain In Pictures Publishers, Bahamas.
E 34,173, S 27,589, U 6,584, R 6,467

Francis Sydney Smythe, mountain climber and writer, b 6 July 1900, d 27 June 1949, ed Berkhamstead School and Farraday House Electrical Engineering College. His career is referred to in Part 1 pp 54-55. WW DNB.

23 English Novelists. Elizabeth Bowen
Literature and Belles Lettres. 8 cp, 16 bw.
Pub 1942. O 29 March and 19 April, TLS 16 May. 2nd imp 1945, 3rd 1946, 4th 1947. Reprinted for FOB.
Included in OV *Impressions of English Literature* (134).
Undated edit pub Britain In Pictures Publishers, Bahamas.
E 40,403, S 46,691, U oversold, R 5,572.

Elizabeth Dorothea Cole Bowen CBE, novelist, b 7 June 1899, d 22 February 1973, ed Downe House Kent. Published 27 books, mainly novels, of which *The Heat of the Day* 1947 was her greatest commercial success. Wrote a history of her family and their house *Bowen's Court* in 1942. She was brought up by a committee of aunts from the age of 13 after the death of her mother who had separated from her father six years earlier. She described herself as 'farouche' (sullen, shy), but had a love of talk, a talent for intimacy, and a hankering after the bizarre and the vulgar. WW DNB CA

24 English Social Services. Sir George Newman
Science, Medicine and Engineering. 8 cp, 21 bw including 12 ph.
Pub 1941. O 29 March and 19 April, TLS 18 July.
An edition translated into Italian was published in 1944 as *L'Assistenza Sociale in Inghilterra* with some resetting to accommodate explanatory footnotes and the transfer of the bibliography from the back to the front.
E 13,771, S 13,567, U 204.

Sir George Newman KCB GBE, public servant, b 23 October 1870, d 26 May 1948, ed Bootham School, King's College London and Edinburgh University. Started working life as a lecturer in public health at St Bartholomew's Medical School, then medical officer posts in local government. After the publication of his report on infant mortality 1906, he became Chief Medical Officer to the Board of Education the following year; and Chief Medical Officer to the Ministry of Health in 1919 following his war work on the health of munition workers. He wrote a series of brilliant annual reports, 15 to the Ministry of Health and 26 to the Ministry of Education, which had an enduring impact on public health. He was one of the inspirations behind the foundation of the Postgraduate Medical School of London and the London School of Hygiene and Tropical Medicine. An active Quaker, he was chairman of the Friends' Ambulance Unit, which served on the Front in the First War, and edited anonymously the *Friends' Quarterly Examiner*. He wrote his BP volume at the age of 70. WW DNB

25 British Cartoonists, Caricaturists and Comic Artists. David Low
Art and Craftsmanship. 8 cp, 25 bw, 3 tp.
Pub 1942. TLS 11 July.
Included in OV *Aspects Of British Art* (138).
This is one of the three volumes to use a bw print on the dust-jacket and the cover instead of the usual white stylised design. (For others see entries 34 and 105).
E 19,384, S 19,655, U oversold.

Sir David Alexander Cecil Low, cartoonist, b 7 April 1891, d 19 September 1963. He

The Books 83

was born in New Zealand and left school at the age of 11 to be educated at home. He drew cartoons for newspapers in New Zealand and Australia before coming to London in 1919 to be political cartoonist for *The Star* until 1926 when he joined the *Evening Standard*. His new contract stated that he was '... to have complete freedom in the selection and treatment of subject matter.' His anti-fascist cartoons caused the newspaper to be banned in Italy and Germany and he was '... reliably informed that he had been included in the Gestapo list for elimination.' He left for the *Daily Herald* in 1949 and stayed there until he retired. His cartoon characters included Col Blimp and the TUC carthorse. WW DNB CA

26 New Zealand. Ngaio Marsh and R.M. Burden
BC, 12 cp, 27 bw.
Pub 1942. O 29 March and 19 April, TLS 25 April. The spelling of Mr Burdon's surname on the title page is incorrect, and his name was omitted from the dust-jacket and cover.
Included in OV *The British Commonwealth and Empire* (133).
E 18,464, S 17,087, U 1,377

Dame Edith Ngaio Marsh, b 23 April 1899, d 18 February 1982, ed St Margaret's College and Canterbury University College School of Art in New Zealand. From 1920-23 she was an actress and producer with a touring company performing Shakespeare and from 1928-32 worked as an interior designer in London. She then returned to New Zealand where she wrote the detective stories, usually with the character of Inspector Alleyn, which made her famous. DNB CA

Randal Mathews Burdon, b 4 August 1896, d 29 November 1965, farmer and author, born in England but ed in New Zealand at Waiki School Winchester and Christ's College Christchurch. At the age of 18 he enlisted and served in France and Italy, being wounded and awarded the Military Cross for bravery. He served in India between 1918-22 in the 13th Bengal Lancers. He then became a sheep farmer in South Canterbury until 1948 and combined his farming with writing, mainly history and biography including three volumes on *New Zealand Notables*. Mr Burdon's daughter, Juliet Hobbs, sent me correspondence between her father and Ngaio Marsh, exchanged when they were writing their BC volume on New Zealand, which is referred to in Part 1 pp 30, 34 and 50.

27 British Merchant Adventurers. Maurice Collis
History and Achievement. 8 cp, 24 bw including 3 tp. Foreword by Walter Turner.
Pub 1942. O 29 March and 19 April, TLS 18 April.
Included in OV *British Adventure* (137).
E 18,554, S 18,269, U 285.

Maurice Collis, public servant and writer, b 10 January 1889, d 12 January 1973, ed Rugby School and Corpus Christi College Oxford. Worked first in the Indian Civil Service and then spent 23 years in Burma where he was a District Magistrate and Excise Commissioner. After his retirement in 1936 he began his literary career, writing histories, novels and biographies including *Siamese White* 1936, *She Was a Queen*, 1937, an autobiography *Trials In Burma* 1938 and, much later in 1966, a biography of Sir Stamford Raffles, one of the heroes of his BP volume whose achievements ironically, as a result of the Japanese invasion of Singapore, had all but disappeared by the time the book was published in the spring of 1942. WW CA

28 The English Church. The Bishop of Chichester, G.K.A. Bell
Education and Religion. 8 cp, 20 bw.
Pub 1942. TLS 15 August.
E 17,267, S 16,859, U 408.

The Rt Revd George Kennedy Allen Bell, clergyman, b 4 February 1883, d 3 October 1958, ed Westminster School, Christ Church College Oxford and Wells Theological College. He was a curate in Leeds 1907-10, lecturer at Christ Church 1910-14, Chaplain to the Archbishop of Canterbury 1914-24, Dean of Canterbury 1924-29 and Bishop of Chichester 1929-58. He was a 'social' bishop, involving himself in employment matters, famine relief, and the Workers' Educational Association. During the 1939-45 war he was a controversial figure, refusing to identify the German people with National Socialism and condemning allied bombing of German cities. This independence was thought to have been a factor in his not being appointed Archbishop of Canterbury when the Archbishopric fell vacant in 1942 and 1944. He was controversial too in other ways, arranging in 1928 the first dramatic performance in an English cathedral since the middle ages with Masefield's *The Coming of Christ* and encouraging T.S. Eliot to write *Murder in the Cathedral* for performance at the Canterbury Festival in 1935. WW DNB

29 English Women. Edith Sitwell
Social Life and Character. 8 cp, 28 bw including 7 tp and 1 v on p5 not listed.
Pub 1942 (Fifoot's bibliography of the Sitwells says 22 June with 17,000 copies printed).
See Part 1 p53 for reference to correspondence about her book.
E 19,458, S 19,025, U 433.

Dame Edith Louisa Sitwell, poet, critic, personality, b 7 September 1887, d 9 December 1964, ed at home. She became a public figure in June 1923 with the performance of Walton's *Facade*, speaking her poems to his music through a megaphone poked between the theatre curtains. Her personal appearance was as striking as her personality, and both contributed to later fame as a television celebrity. In addition to her many poems and other writings she wrote a book on *English Eccentrics* in 1933, a group to which she certainly belonged. WW DNB CA

30 English Children. Sylvia Lynd
Social Life and Character. 12 cp, 28 bw.
Pub 1942. TLS 4 July.
E 19,571, S 19,329, U 242.

Sylvia Lynd, poet and author, b 1888, d 21 February 1952, ed St Alfred's School, London, the Slade School and the Academy of Dramatic Art. She wrote a number of novels and books of poetry including *The Chorus* 1916, *The Thrush and the Jay* 1917, and *The Goldfinders* 1920; edited *The Children's Omnibus* 1932; and published an autobiography just before her death. WW

The Books

31 Life Among the English. Rose Macaulay
Social Life and Character. 8 cp, 27 bw including 3 tp and 1 v.
Pub 1942. TLS 17 October. 2nd imp 1946. Reprinted for FOB.
E 50,540, S 61,636, U oversold, R 861.

Dame Rose Macaulay, author, b 1 August 1881, d 30 October 1958, ed in early years by her parents in Genoa and then in Oxford High School and Somerville College Oxford. She wrote 24 novels, mainly before 1914 and in the period between the wars, and, after 1945, a number of travel books. *The Towers of Trebizond* which won the James Tait Black Memorial prize was published in 1956. She also wrote poetry and a biography of Milton and contributed regularly to the weeklies and *The Observer* newspaper. Three volumes of her letters were published after her death. *The Times* obituary described her as 'an author of lively and ironic intelligence, wide scholarship and fastidious wit. Everything she touched took on part of her own vitality. Even the hardly tried succession of cars in which she terrified her friends acquired an almost human responsiveness to the dash of her approach. Nothing frightened her. Just as she made a habit of swimming in the coldest water ... at the most unpromising times of the year, she used her remarkable intellectual faculties in every climate of opinion.' During the 1939-45 war she worked as a voluntary ambulance driver for three years and lost all her belongings when her flat was bombed. Perhaps she was reflecting this personal experience when she wrote in her BP volume about bombs tearing homes to pieces (see Part 1 pp 44-45) WW DNB CA.

32 British Dramatists. Graham Greene
English Literature and Belles Lettres. 8 cp, 25 bw including 3 tp.
Pub 1942. TLS 24, O 27 October.
Included in OV *Impressions of English Literature* (134).
E 14,526, S 14,177, U 349.

Graham Greene OM CH, novelist, b 2 October 1904, d 3 April 1991, ed Berkhamstead School and Balliol College Oxford. According to a letter to his mother, quoted by Norman Sherry in his biography (p 108, vol 2, pub Jonathan Cape 1994), Greene wrote his BIP book without the use of reference books whilst travelling by boat to West Africa between December 1941 and February 1942. By this time he had already written 16 books, mainly novels, including *Stamboul Train, Brighton Rock* and *The Power and the Glory*. WW CA

33 British Rebels and Reformers. Harry Roberts
Social Life and Character. 8 cp, 17 bw, 1 v.
Pub 1942. TLS 3 October.
E 18,578, S 18,171, U 407. See also entry 59.

Dr Harry Roberts, medical practitioner, social reformer and gardener, b 1871, d 12 November 1946, ed Miss Edney's School for Young Ladies in Bishop Lydeard, Berrington's Preparatory School in Taunton, Queen's College Taunton, University College Bristol and St Mary's Hospital and Medical School, London; he was a prize-winner in all but the first. He practised medicine in Cornwall and Stepney, worked as a school teacher and lecturer, was medical correspondent of various newspapers and wrote on medicine and gardening, including the BP volume on *English Gardens* (59). He retained a connection all his life with the labour movement. His books included works on abortion, euthanasia, social and health policy, and religion as well as *The Chronicle of a Cornish Garden*. WW

34   British Romantic Artists. John Piper
Art and Craftsmanship. 12 cp, 28 bw including 3 t.
Pub 1942. TLS 12, O 27 December. 2nd imp 1946.
Included in OV *Aspects of British Art* (138).
One of only three volumes to have a print reproduced on upper dust-jacket and cover instead of the usual stylised design. (For others see entries 25 and 105). The title was first advertised as *English Romantic Painting*.
E 32,857, S 30,146, U 2,711, R 2,102.

John Egerton Christmas Piper CH, painter and writer, b 13 December 1903, d 28 June 1992, ed Epsom College and the Royal College of Art. He was a man of exceptionally varied talents. A profile in the *Sunday Times* of 9 December 1951 records him as having been '... at one time or another a pianist in a dance band, a Trustee of the Tate Gallery, a theatre-proprietor, a performer on television, a member of the Oxford Diocesan Board, an editor of guide books, and a stage designer... but never has Piper ceased to be first and last a painter.' His obituary in *The Times* mentioned even more, including stained glass and tapestry, pointing out that he scaled a separate height in each decade. He worked for the War Artists Commission and also *Recording Britain*. John Rothenstein in *Modern English Painters* (Macdonald 1984) describes his BP volume as '... a short but informative and lively book' in which 'Piper's own attitude to the arts is more clearly manifest... than in any of his other writings. A friend pleased him by saying, "I know it by heart."' See Part 1 pp 49 and 52 for other contemporary comments about his book. WW

35   British Ports and Harbours. Leo Walmsley
Topographical History. 8 cp, 23 bw including 1 v.
Pub 1942. TLS 30 January 1943. 2nd imp 1946.
Included in OV *The Englishman's Country* (135).
E 32,058, S 28,473, U 3,585, R 2,475.

Leo Walmsley MC, author, b 29 September 1892, d 8 June 1966, ed as a scholarship boy in the local High School near Robin Hood's Bay in Yorkshire. Teacher and journalist before enlisting in the 1914-18 war. Served in East Africa, mentioned in despatches four times, awarded the MC. After being invalided out of the forces he began his career as a writer. He wrote 13 books before his BP volume, including *Three Fevers* in 1932, which became the film *Turn of the Tide*, and the four *Bramblewick* novels which describe growing up in Yorkshire. Nearly all his 23 books have a strong biographical element, including his BP volume and the officially commissioned *Fishermen At War* in 1941. His BP book is one of those in the series which seems at first sight to be unpromising, but turns out to be a treasure-house of information and good writing. The first seven pages are an evocation of childhood in Whitby which rivals many of Dickens's descriptions, especially the account of a visit to Liverpool and a day spent at the docks in defiance of an aunt and uncle whose idea of a good time for children was regular periods of prayer. There is a Walmsley Society in Halifax which was set up to make better known the writings of this neglected author; a reading of *British Ports and Harbours* demonstrates how worthwhile their objective is. WW CA

36 The Birds of Britain. James Fisher
Topographical History. 12 cp, 26 bw including 1 tp.
Pub 1942. O 6, TLS 12 December. 3rd and 4th imp 1947. Reprinted for FOB.
Included in OV *Nature in Britain* (136).
Was first advertised with Professor Julian Huxley as joint author.
E 95,534, S 84,218, U 11,316, R 5,898.

James Maxwell McConnell Fisher, ornithologist, writer, broadcaster, b 3 September 1912, d 25 September 1970, ed Eton and Magdalen College Oxford. Ornithologist on the Spitzbergen expedition of 1936, Assistant Curator Zoological Society London, 1936-39, Treasurer then Secretary British Trust for Ornithology 1938-44, Natural History Editor at Collins 1946-54 and founder of their New Naturalist series. He is said to have made over 1,000 broadcasts on natural history. His BP volume sold more than any other. WW DNB CA

37 British Orientalists. A.J. Arberry
Literature and Belles Lettres. 8 cp, 20 bw including 2 v.
Pub 1943. O 28 February, TLS 10 April.
E 10,865, S 10,689, U 176.

Professor Arthur John Arberry, orientalist, b 12 May 1905, d 2 October 1969, ed Portsmouth Grammar School and Pembroke College Cambridge. Head of Department of Classics University of Cairo 1932, Assistant Librarian India Office 1934-39, Ministry of Information 1939-44, Professor of Persian and of Arabic, University of London and Head of Middle East Department in the School of Oriental and African Studies 1944-46, and Sir Thomas Adams Professor of Arabic Cambridge 1947-69. He published over 60 books including a translation of *The Koran* and two versions of *The Rubaiyat of Omar Khayyam*. He began to learn Arabic at school and after completing a 'safe' degree in classics to ensure employment, he then took firsts in oriental languages. He complains that oriental studies in Britain have never recovered from Macaulay's dismissive and ignorant assertion that oriental literature was worth a single shelf of the classics of Europe. There is a poignant reference in his BP book to (Sir) Anthony Eden then, in 1943, Foreign Secretary. Eden had studied at Oxford under the Arabic scholar D.S. Margoliouth and Arberry records '... the hope of every orientalist that Mr Eden, whose brilliant academic career promised so much for Islamic studies, may find the time after ... the war ... to make those contributions to Arabic and Persian scholarship which Gladstone made to Greek ...'. Professor Arberry could hardly have foreseen Eden's actual contribution later as Prime Minister when he directed the invasion of Egypt in 1956. WW DNB CA

38 British Craftsmen. T. Hennell
Art and Craftsmanship. 8 cp, 29 bw including 1 v.
Pub 1943. O 28 February, TLS 6 March. Author styled Thomas Hennell on spine and T. Hennell on title page. 2nd imp 1946.
Included in OV *British Craftsmanship* (139).
E 29,385, S 29,315, U 70.

Thomas Barclay Hennell, painter, teacher and writer, b 16 April 1903 d November (?) 1945, ed Hildersham House School Broadstairs, Bradfield School and The Regent Street Polytechnic School of Art. After teaching from 1926 until about 1930, he concentrated on his books and paintings. He was one of 95 artists selected to make a pictorial record during the 1939-45 war of the changing face of Britain; this was the Pilgrim Trust project which published some of the paintings as *Recording Britain*, and included many of Thomas Hennell's works. Writing in volume 3 of *Recording Britain,* Arnold Palmer the editor comments that Hennell's painting of the Tithe House, Greet Manor Farm, Winchcomb in Gloucestershire, must have been one of his last pictures. Palmer describes him as 'a man of boundless curiosity and precise knowledge of many and varied matters'. In his book on *Modern English Painters*, Sir John Rothenstein says Hennell was a man virtually without ambition and highly individual, not linked to any school or clique. He was first commissioned as a war artist in June 1943 to record the war in Iceland. He returned to England, recorded preparations for the D-day landings, landed in Normandy in June 1944 and advanced into Europe. In February 1945 he was recalled and attached to the RAF to record the war in India, Burma and the East Indies. Some time in November Hennell was captured by Indonesian nationalists. He was last seen armed with a sten gun guarding civilians who had taken refuge in a hotel in what was then called Batavia, and was reported missing, later presumed killed. He was forty-two. He wrote a number of other books including a novel *The Witnesses*, 1938, which includes an account of his madness (he was diagnosed as schizophrenic) and gradual recovery.

39 The Story of Ireland. Sean O'Faolain
Topographical History. 8 cp, 22 bw.
Pub 1943. TLS 18 December. 2nd imp 1946.
(Another volume on Ireland, to be written by Prof. Walter Starkie, was planned as part of the British Commonwealth series, but was not published.)
E 29,188, S 25,986, U 3,202.

Sean O'Faolain (born John Whelan), writer, b 22 February 1900, d 21 April 1991, ed National University of Ireland and Harvard University. He was active in the IRA during the Irish war of Independence and took up arms against the Government of the new Irish State. He became disillusioned with Irish Governments, changed his name to Sean O'Faolain and was active in the movement for a totally independent, gaelic speaking, Ireland. In 1940 he founded an influential literary journal called *The Bell* of which he was editor until 1946. He analysed his society in harsh terms, seeking the freedom of the individual against the repressions of the Irish Catholic middle class. *The Bell* provided a platform for all those who were out of sympathy with the orthodoxies of nationalist Ireland. His *Times'* obituary assessed his real significance as his response to post-revolutionary Irish society which he enriched by staying and protesting rather than leaving. His first book, *Midsummer Madness* published in 1932, was banned as obscene by the Irish Government, deepening his disillusion with Ireland's new order. He was the biographer of Hugh O'Neil Earl of Tyrone, Wolf Tone, Constance Markievicz and Eamon De Valera and wrote many novels. In the 1980s three volumes of his stories were published. His autobiography *Vive Moi* was published by Sinclair-Stevenson in 1994 and in the same year there was a biography by Maurice Harmon published by Constable. CA

40 The British Colonial Empire. Noel Sabine
BC, 8 cp, 26 bw including 14 photographs, 2 v and 1 map.
Pub 1943. TLS 22 May.
The half-title reads Britain in Pictures, The British People in Pictures, although it is clearly part of the British Commonwealth series and is included in the OV *The British Commonwealth and Empire* (133).
E 18,334, S 17,915, U 319.

Noel John Barrington Sabine, d 8 February 1972. Nothing known other than biographical details on the dust-jacket referring to his membership of the Administrative service in Kenya and work in the Colonial office, and a notice of his death in *The Times* which records that he was a JP for Essex.

41 Britain and the Middle East. Sir Ronald Storrs
Not published.

42 Children's Verse
Not published.

43 Coleridge. Dorothy Wellesley (Editor)
EP, 80 p, 4 cp, 17 bw
Pub 1942. No review in O or TLS. An errata slip recorded five errors.
E, S, U, no figures. See also entries 7, 8, 19, 20 and 44.

44 Wordsworth. Dorothy Wellesley (Editor)
EP, 80 p, 4 cp, 17 bw.
Pub 1942. No review in O or TLS. An errata slip recorded three errors.
E, S, U, no figures. See also entries 7, 8, 19, 20 and 43.

45 British Trade Unions. Sir Walter Citrine
Social Life and Character. 8 cp, 23 bw including 1 tp.
Pub 1942. TLS 8 August.
E 9,536, S 9,598, U oversold.

Walter McLennon Citrine, First Baron Citrine, electrician, trade union leader, manager, b 22 August 1887, d 22 January 1983, ed at elementary school, trained as electrician, taught himself economics, accountancy and shorthand. He became a trade union official, then joined the TUC in 1924 and became its General Secretary in 1926, the year of the General Strike. He turned down an offer by Ramsay Macdonald of a peerage in 1930, and also an invitation from Churchill to join the coalition government in 1941, but later accepted appointments by the Labour Government, first to the National Coal Board and then, in 1947, to the chairmanship of the Central Electricity Authority which he held for ten years. He was a great administrator, creative but ruthlessly self-disciplined. A profile of 6 June 1943 in *The Observer* described him as a man of moderate views, a pillar of democratic rectitude, the perfect Secretary, punctilious, precise and always right in his facts. He built up the TUC so that it could work with any government. He could be a martinet, but he also had considerable personal charm and in his lighter moments he played the cornet, loved opera and community singing and was interested in palmistry. WW DNB CA

46 Fairs, Circuses and Music Halls. M. Willson Disher
Social Life and Character. 8 cp, 27 bw including 5 tp. Introductory Note on Fairs by C. Henry Warren (author of *English Cottages and Farmhouses*). (128)
Pub 1942. TLS 19 December.
E 16,536, S 16,114, U 422.

Maurice Willson Disher, author and critic, b 10 January 1893, d 24 November 1969, ed very little because of long illness. He became music hall critic of the *Standard* and the *Evening Standard* in 1911, then drama critic from 1912 to 1921, music hall and film critic of *The Observer* 1927-28, drama critic of the *Daily Mail* 1933-36, and a contributor to *The Times* and the TLS from 1937-53. He wrote novels, histories, plays and radio programmes, all usually connected with the circus and music halls or other forms of public amusement. WW CA

47 British Engineers. Metius Chappell
Science, Medicine and Engineering 8 cp, 27 bw.
Pub 1942. O 28 February, TLS 24 April.
E 15,046, S 17,838, U oversold.

Metius Chappell: nothing known other than information on dust-jacket describing him as '... a brilliant young Canadian writer ... a lecturer in economic history and ... a specialist in the eighteenth and nineteenth centuries.' Sheila Shannon has a copy of his book signed by him as John Buckatzsch (Metius Chappell), but knows nothing of the reason behind the use of a pen-name.

48 English Cities and Small Towns. John Betjeman
Topographical History. 8 cp, 31 bw.
Pub 1943. Rev. TLS 27, O 28 February. 2nd and 3rd imp 1943, 4th 1947. Reprinted for FOB.
Included in OV, *The Englishman's Country* (135).
E 45,817, S 38,108, U 7,709, R 1958.

Sir John Betjeman CBE, poet, writer on architecture, broadcaster, b 28 August 1906, d 19 May 1984, ed Dragon School Oxford and Marlborough College from which he was rusticated for failing Divinity. He worked as a preparatory school master, assistant editor of the Architectural Review in 1930 and film critic of the *Evening Standard* in 1933, after which he concentrated on his poetry, other writing, broadcasting and on such projects as the Shell Guides on which he co-operated with John Piper (see entry 34). He was Poet Laureate 1972-84. Philip Larkin said of him in *Required Writing*, 1983 'He offers us something we cannot find in any other writer — a gaiety, a sense of the ridiculous, an affection for human beings and how and where they live, a vivid and vivacious portrait of mid-twentieth-century English life.' All these qualities shine out of his delightful BP volume. WW DNB CA

The Books

49   British Historians. E. L. Woodward
Literature and Belles Lettres. 8 cp, 21 bw including 1 v.
Pub 1943. TLS 15 May with subsequent correspondence on 3 July.
Included in OV *Impressions of English Literature* (134).
E 10,883, S 10,611, U 272.

Sir Ernest Llewelyn Woodward, historian, b 14 May 1890, d 11 March 1971, ed Merchant Taylor's School and Corpus Christi College Oxford. He served in the first world war from 1915-18 and was invalided home from Salonika, after which the Foreign Office invited him to write a short handbook on the Congress of Berlin 1878, as preparation for the Versailles Peace Conference. He was a history master at Eton School and lecturer at New College Oxford, 1922-39. He was one of the first people to warn against appeasing Hitler, which he did in a letter to *The Times* 27 March 1933. From 1939-45 he worked at the Foreign Office on British Foreign Policy documents of the period 1919-39. He became Professor of International Relations 1944-47 and then Professor of Modern History 1947-51 at Oxford. He did not feel at home in post-war Britain which he regarded as too parochial and he moved to the United States of America where he became a Professor at the Institute for Advanced Studies, Princeton, 1951-62. WW DNB CA

50   British Soldiers. S. H. F. Johnston
History and Achievement. 8 cp, 25 bw.
Pub 1944. TLS 17 March 1945. (The number indicates that it was planned for publication in 1943; whilst the length of time between the stated date of publication and the review indicates that it probably was not published until 1945.)
Included in OV *British Adventure* (137).
E 18,448, S 18,393, U 55.

Major Samuel Henry Fergus Johnston, university teacher, b 2 November 1908, d 16 February 1991 (an obituary in the *Aberystwyth News* gives 16th, but another reference gives 13th), ed King George V Grammar School Southport and Exeter College Oxford. In 1934 he was appointed as a temporary Assistant Lecturer at the University College of Wales Aberystwyth and was promoted successively to Lecturer, Senior Lecturer, Reader and, in 1967, Professor. During the war of 1939-45 he served as a civilian instructor and obtained a commission in the Aberystwyth contingent of the Senior Training Corps, eventually commanding the unit with the rank of Major until its disbandment. Many of his publications were about the wars of William III and Queen Anne and also Wellington's Peninsular War campaigns about which he became an expert, although he never produced the promised definitive work. Between 1943-47 he wrote regularly on military matters for *The Spectator*.

51   The English at Table. John Hampson
Social Life and Character. 8 cp, 25 bw.
Pub 1944. TLS 3 March 1945. (Again, as with 50, the dates are rather odd.) 2nd imp 1946.
E 25,635, S 25,769, U oversold.

John Hampson-Simpson (the shorter version was his pen-name), caterer and author, b 1900, d 29 December 1955. He spent most of his life in the Midlands, in his early years as an employee in the catering trade. He used this experience in his books such as *Saturday*

Night at the Greyhound published in 1931, a study of public house life in a colliery district of the North Midlands, and in numerous short stories and radio scripts. One coloured illustration alone, that of the weekly food ration for two people in 1941 opposite page 40, makes his BIP book worthwhile.

52 Wild Life of Britain. F. Fraser Darling
Natural History. 8 cp, 29 bw including 1 v.
Pub 1943. TLS 12 June. 3rd imp 1947. Reprinted for FOB.
Included in Ov, *Nature in Britain* (136).
E 79,024, S 56,822, U 22,262, R 8,805. (See also entry 21.)

53 British Polar Explorers. Admiral Sir Edward Evans
History and Achievement. 8 cp, 19 bw including 1 v.
Pub 1943. O 22 August, TLS 4 September. 2nd imp 1946. Included in OV, *British Adventure* (137).
E 32,850, S 26,265, U 6,585, R 6,042.

Edward Ratcliffe Garth Russell Evans, First Baron Mountevans CB KCB, sailor, b 28 October 1881 (although one reference book gives 1880), d 20 August 1957, ed first at Merchant Taylors School from which he was expelled for truancy, then at Kenley, a school for troublesome boys where he was very happy, then Warwick House School, Maida Vale, and finally the 'Worcester' a mercantile marine training ship. His part in Scott's Antarctic expeditions and later career has been described in Part 1 pp 53-54. Admiral Evans was a man who revelled in publicity and whose adventurous life ensured that he was often in the public eye. In addition to his BP volume he wrote *South With Scott* 1921, *Adventurous Life* 1946 and *Happy Adventurer*, 1951. There was also a biography *Evans of the Broke* by Reginald Pound published in 1963. WW DNB

54 English Conversation — British Conversationalists. Lord David Cecil — Lettice Fowler
Not published. Advertised at different times as English Conversation by Lord David Cecil and British Conversationalists by Lettice Fowler.

55 English Diaries and Journals. Kate O'Brien
Literature and Belles Lettres. 8 cp, 19 bw including 3 v.
Pub 1943. No reviews, although included in TLS reviews index for December 1943. 2nd imp 1943, 3rd imp 1947.
Included in OV, *Impressions of English Literature* (134).
E 39,999, S 31,256, U 8,743, R 8,146.

Kate O'Brien, playwright, novelist, critic, b 3 December 1897, d 13 August 1974, ed Laurel Hill Convent, Limerick, and University College Dublin. She worked in the foreign languages department of *The Manchester Guardian* and was then a school-mistress and a governess in Spain before her first play, *Distinguished Villa*, was produced in 1926, and her first novel, *Without My Cloak*, in 1931, the latter winning both the Hawthornden and James Tait Black Memorial prizes. Her novel of convent life, *The Land of Spices* published in 1941 was banned in Ireland. WW DNB CA

The Books

56 British Biographies. Rebecca West
Not published.

57 British Horses and Ponies. Lady Wentworth
Country Life and Sport. 8 cp, 26 bw (counting page 47 as five illustrations).
Pub 1944. TLS 1 April with subsequent correspondence on 6 and 13 May and 17 June.
2nd imp and 3rd 1944, 4th 1947. Reprinted for FOB.
The title above is the one used on the title page. However, the title on both upper dust-jacket and upper cover is *Horses of Britain*, whilst on the inside of the upper dust-jacket it is *Horses and Ponies of Britain*.
E 56,567, S 47,945, U 8622, R 4,520.

Judith Anne Dorothea Blunt-Lytton, 16th Baroness Wentworth, (the Barony was created in 1529, she took the surname Blunt-Lytton by deed-poll in 1904 and inherited the title by special remainder in 1917), horse-breeder, b 1873, d 8 August 1957. As well as being an expert on horse breeding, she was a world tennis champion, and a poet and painter. She took issue with the TLS reviewer who had questioned her rejection of the theory that there were some native English mares. This exchange went on until 17 June with other readers joining in, but Lady Wentworth held her ground. Her fame as a breeder and a woman of firm views clearly lives on; Bruce Chatwin in his book *What Am I Doing Here?*, pub 1989, refers to the Chinese desire for Horses from Heaven which sweated blood, a phenomenon attributed by some to a parasitic insect, '... but Lady Wentworth, who bred the finest Arabians in England, once had a horse that sweated blood. And she would have been the first to spot a parasite.' See also Part 1 p51-52 for other biographical details. WW

58 British Seamen. David Mathew
History and Achievement. 8 cp, 26 bw including 2 v.
Pub 1943. TLS 21 August. 2nd imp 1943.
Included in OV, *British Adventure* (137).
E 28,585, S 27,858, U 727, R 165.

The Most Revd David Mathew, priest and scholar, b 15 January 1902, d 12 December 1975, ed Osborne, Dartmouth Naval College and Balliol College Oxford. He was a midshipman from 1918-19 before going to Balliol where he continued to carry out research for many years whilst he was successively an Assistant Priest in Cardiff 1930-34, Chaplain to London University catholics 1934-44 and Bishop Auxiliary of Westminster 1938-46. He was appointed Archbishop of Apamea in Bythymia in 1946 and was Apostolic Delegate to British Colonies in Africa until 1953 when, on refusing further preferment, he returned to England and became Bishop in Ordinary to HM Forces. He wrote several histories, mainly on naval subjects, but also on the reformation, the renaissance, and the celtic peoples. It is interesting that two of the most exciting martial books in the BIP series, his own and that on Battlefields (78), were written respectively by an archbishop and a woman. WW DNB CA

59 English Gardens. Harry Roberts
Country Life and Sport. 8 cp, 23 bw.
Pub 1944. TLS 27 May. 2nd imp 1944, 3rd 1947. Reprinted for FOB.

Included in OV, *The Englishman's Country.* (135)
E 44,481, S 41,176, U 3,305, R 2,912. See also entry 33.

60 British Philosophers. Kenneth Matthews
Literature and Belles Lettres. 8 cp, 14 bw including 1 v.
Pub 1943. TLS 26 February 1944.
Included in OV, *Impressions of English Literature* (134).
E 15,725, S 15,756, U oversold. See also entry 127.

Kenneth Albert Matthews, university teacher, b 21 May 1908, ed Kingswood School Bath and Peterhouse College Cambridge. Assistant master at Spetsae School in the Gulf of Nauplia, Greece 1931-32 then an author and journalist. He wrote several books about Greek life including *Greek Salad: an autobiography of Greek travel,* 1935; translations from Greek literature; and some novels including *Aleko* in 1934 and *Celia Employed* in 1937. See also Part 1 pp 55-57 for comments on his book.

61 Women's Institutes. Cicely McCall
Social Life and Character. 8 cp, 22 bw including 2 v and 18 photographs.
Pub 1943. TLS 3 July.
E 17,927, S 17,486, U 441.

Cicely McCall: nothing known other than information on dust-jacket which records that she had wide experience of Women's Institutes (WIs) all over the country. Her fascinating account of WIs in war-time is referred to in Part 1 pp 43-44.

62 The Story of Wales. Rhys Davies
Topographical History. 8 cp, 30 bw including 4 v.
Pub 1943. TLS 14, O 15 August. 2nd imp 1943, 3rd 1947.
E 39,595, S 36,196, U 3,399, R 2,443.

Rhys Davies OBE, novelist, b 9 November 1903, d 21 August 1978, (the DNB gives his birth date as 9 November 1901, but this must be an error as later information in the same article is compatible with 1903), ed Porth County School. He left for London in 1918 at the age of 15 and by the time his BP volume was issued he had published 13 works, mainly novels. *The Story of Wales* was advertised first with Dylan Thomas as author, a choice that would have scandalised Welsh puritans, but his replacement by Rhys Davies was scarcely more likely to please. Rhys Davies's recreations in *Who's Who* are given as the theatre, living in London and cultivating ruined characters. In the magazine *New Coterie* he published *Carnal Stories,* and following a visit to D.H. Lawrence at Bandol he smuggled into Britain the typescript of Lawrence's proscribed poems *Pansies.* In his autobiography he wrote that he had '... set about ridding Anglo-Welsh writing of flannel and bringing some needed flesh tints to it.' See Part 1 p 50 for comments on his text. WW DNB CA

63 British Clubs. Bernard Darwin
Social Life and Character. 8 cp, 20 bw including 2 v.
Pub 1943. TLS 20 November. 2nd imp 1943, 3rd (revised) 1946.
E 36,431, S 26,254, U 10,087, R 7,197. See also entry 107.

The Books

Bernard Richard Meirion Darwin CBE, writer, b 7 September 1876, d 18 October 1961, ed Summerfields School Oxford, Eton, and Trinity College Cambridge. He was called to the Bar in 1903, but by 1907 was writing occasional pieces for the *Evening Standard, The Times* and *Country Life*, and in 1908 began to devote himself full-time to writing about golf (see entry 107 for golfing career). His DNB biographer says that 'It was as though he deliberately turned his back on the scholarship and literary talent by which he was surrounded in his family' — his father was the botanist Sir Francis Darwin and his great-grandfather was Charles Darwin. Apart from golf and clubs, his other great loves were the writings of Charles Dickens and cricket, and in the Great Lives series he wrote biographies of Dickens and W. G

64 The Londoner. Lady Nicholson
Social Life and Character. 8 cp, 20 bw.
Pub 1944. TLS 1 July. Author styled Dorothy Nicholson on cover and Lady Nicholson on title page. 2nd imp revised 1946.
E 29,220, S 28,028, U 1,192.

Lady Dorothy Nicholson (formerly Lady Brooke), author: nothing known other than previous publications *Private Letters, Pagan and Christian* and *Pilgrims Were They All* listed on dust-jacket.

65 Wild Flowers in Britain. Geoffrey Grigson
Natural History. 12 cp (the rosebay willowherb facing page 33 is not listed on the title page of the first edition), 22 bw.
Pub 1944. O 9 April, TLS 27 May. 2nd imp and 3rd 1944, 4th 1947.
Reprinted for FOB.
Included in OV, *Nature in Britain* (136).
E 63,273, S 60, 574, U 2,699, R 14,859. (The remaindered figure does not make sense. A possible explanation is that the figures for 1951-52 recorded by Collins in their letter to Adprint of 27 May 1953 consist of a mixture of remaindered figures and additional volumes published for the FOB. See schedule of sales p 120-123.)

Geoffrey Edward Harvey Grigson, poet, man of letters, critic, botanist, ornithologist, b 2 March 1905, d 28 November 1985, ed minor public school in Leatherhead, and St Edmund's Hall Oxford which he regarded as profitless, taking a third class in English in 1927. He had a very unhappy childhood, being the seventh male child born when his father was 59 and his mother 42. Three of his brothers were killed in the first world war and three in the second. His childhood is described in his autobiography *The Crest on the Silver*, 1950. He was a journalist with the *Yorkshire Post* and then with *The Morning Post* of which he became Literary Editor. He founded and edited *New Verse*, 1933-39, which was well known for publishing the poetry of W. H. Auden and his contemporaries and for Grigson's own '... unsparing and at times ferocious criticism.' (J. Symons) He published anthologies of verse, art criticism, *The Englishman's Flora*, 1955 and the *Shell Country Book*, 1962. WW DNB CA

66 The English Bible. Sir Herbert Grierson
Education and religion. 8 cp, 21 bw including 4 v.
Pub 1943. TLS 18 March 1944. 2nd imp 1943.
Included in OV, *Impressions of English Literature* (134).
E 36,201, S 31,986, U 4,215, R 4,701.

Sir Herbert John Clifford Grierson, scholar, literary critic and writer, b 16 January 1866, d 19 February 1960, ed King's College Aberdeen and Christ Church College Oxford. He then had two unsettled years during which he taught at a girls' school before taking up a lectureship at the University of Aberdeen where he became Professor until 1915. He was appointed in that year as Professor of Rhetoric and English Literature at the University of Edinburgh where he remained until his retirement in 1935. He continued as a Reader until 1939 and went on writing until 1954. His particular love was 17th century writing — his work on Donne and the metaphysical poets in 1912 is a classic. He wrote a biography of Sir Walter Scott and edited a 12 volume edition of Scott's letters. For him, Tyndale remains the great hero of the English Bible and he expresses regret that Tyndale's '... text of 1535 is accessible only in the rather heavy Hexapla of Bagster.' Modern readers, however, have the advantage of David Daniell's edition of Tyndale's New Testament, published in 1989, and of the Old Testament published in 1992, both by Yale University Press. WW DNB CA

67 English Inns. Thomas Burke
Country Life and Sport. 8 cp, 24 bw including 4 v.
Pub 1943. TLS 19 February 1944. 2nd and 3rd imp 1944, 4th 1947.
Included in OV *The Englishman's Country* (135).
E 50,129, S 48,252, U 1,877, R 1,168.

Thomas Burke, literary agent and author, b 1886, d 22 September 1945, wrote extensively on inns and London, especially Chinatown. He also wrote thrillers and his radio play *The Hands of Mr Ottermole* was called by one affidionado 'the greatest mystery story of all time'. WW CA

68 Britain in the Air. Nigel Tangye
History and Achievement. 8 cp, 26 bw.
Pub 1944. TLS 14 October.
Included in OV, *British Adventure* (137).
E 14,420, S 15,018, U oversold.

Wing Commander Nigel Tangye, aeroplane pilot and author, b 24 April 1909, d 2 June 1988, ed Royal Naval College Dartmouth and served in the battleship Valiant. After failing to obtain a transfer to the Fleet Air Arm he left the service to enter civil flying. He was air correspondent for *The Spectator* and *Evening News* and in 1938 wrote *Teach Yourself to Fly*, a book that was adopted by the Air Ministry as the only book officially recommended for study by novice service pilots. He served as a Wing Commander in the RAFVR during the second world war and acted as liaison officer between the RAF and the US Eighth Air Force, for which he was awarded the Legion of Merit. Before the war he served for a time as a secret agent in Spain and after the war was an adviser to the film maker Sir Alexander Korda. His autobiography is called *The House on the Seine*. CA

The Books

69 British Sea Fishermen. Peter F. Anson
History and Achievement. 8 cp, 23 bw including 3 v.
Pub 1944. Rev TLS 9 September.
E 14,536, S 15,116, U oversold.

Peter F. Anson, hermit and painter, b 1879 (1889 in CA), d 10 July 1975, elder son of Admiral Charles Anson, ed Wixenford School and The Architectural Association. In 1910 he entered the Anglican Benedictine monastery on Caldey island and remained with the Order when it joined the Roman Catholic church. He was especially drawn towards Franciscan and Camoldolese hermitages and wrote a book on *The Quest of Solitude*. He became the historian of the monastic communities in the Anglican communion. His other great loves were painting and the sea, a combination which finds wonderful expression in his BP volume. One of his paintings of the Harbour is reproduced opposite page 25 of his volume. CA

70 British Marine Life. C. M. Yonge
Natural History. 8 cp, 26 bw.
Pub 1944. TLS 28 October.
Included in OV, *Nature in Britain* (136).
E 15,939, S 16,411, U oversold.

Sir Charles Maurice Yonge CBE, marine biologist, b 9 December 1899, d 17 March 1986, ed Silcoates School Wakefield, and Edinburgh University. Carnegie Research Scholar 1924-25, Assistant at Marine Biology Association Plymouth 1925-27, Balfour Student Cambridge 1927-29, Leader Great Barrier Reef Expedition 1928-29, Physiologist MBA Plymouth 1930-32, Professor of Zoology University of Bristol 1933-34, Regius Professor of Zoology Glasgow 1944-64, Research Fellow 1965-70. He wrote numerous publications on marine life including *The Sea Shore* in the New Naturalist series. WW

71 British Photographers. Cecil Beaton
Art and Craftsmanship. 4 cp, 8 sepia plates, 20 bw (all photographs).
Pub 1944. O 18 June TLS 1 July. Reprinted in 1987 by Bracken Books.
E 18,827, S 18,798, U 29

Sir Cecil Walter Hardy Beaton CBE, photographer and designer, b 14 January 1904, d 18 January 1980, ed Harrow School and St John's College Cambridge. His ingenious photographic portraits of the Sitwells led to his employment with *Vogue* magazine in London and New York until a disagreement in 1938 resulted in ending his contract. On the outbreak of war he became a notable war photographer. One of the most famous photographs of the war was his picture of a bombed-out child in hospital which was said to have done much to influence American feeling when it was published on the cover of *Life* magazine in September 1940 (reproduced in his BP volume p 37). In addition to being a photographer, he was a stage and film set designer, his work including the set and costumes for both stage and film versions of *My Fair Lady* in 1956 and 1963 respectively, for which film he won an Oscar, his second, having in 1958 won one for his designs for *Gigi*. WW DNB CA

72 British Postage Stamps. S.C. Johnson
Art and Craftsmanship. 8 cp, 25 bw. (This is one of those occasions when the words 'lavishly illustrated' would be accurate; the 8 colour plates contain 102 reproductions of individual stamps or groups of stamps and the 25 black and white plates contain 141 reproductions.)
Pub 1944. TLS 27 May. 2nd imp and 3rd 1944.
E 41,460, S 41,505, U oversold.

Dr S.C. Johnson: no information other than the dust-jacket note that he was an enthusiastic amateur stamp collector.

73 British Maps and Map Makers. Edward Lynam
Science, Medicine and Engineering. 8 cp, 22 bw.
Pub 1944. TLS 23 September. 2nd imp 1944, 3rd revised 1947.
E 36,276, S 33,291, U 2,985, R 3,168.

Edward William O'Flaherty Lynam, Museum Curator, b 18 April 1885, d 29 January 1950, ed Clongoes Wood, Queen's College Cork, Universite de Besancon and the University of London. Between 1914-19 he served in the Royal Irish Regiment, being invalided out; he also served in the Home Guard between 1940-43. In 1910 he was appointed an Assistant Keeper in the British Museum's Department of Printed Books and after the first war as Assistant Superintendent of the Reading room. He became Superintendent of the Map Room in 1931; and was Hon Sec of the Hakluyt Society from 1931-45 and its President from 1945-49. He developed the role of the Map Room significantly and was an authority both on maps and the history of exploration. He wrote several scholarly articles about cartography, exploration, Ireland and Scandinavia; and books on the Fenlands and *The Character of England in Maps*, 1945. WW

74 The British Red Cross. Dermot Morrah
Science, Medicine and Engineering. 4 cp, 8 sp, 10 bw.
Pub 1944. TLS 7 October.
E 19,740, S 20,398, U oversold.

Dermot Michael Macgregor Morrah, journalist, historian, herald, b 26 April 1896, d 30 September 1974, ed Winchester School and New College Oxford. He served in the Royal Engineers 1915-19 and was wounded at Gaza. He was a Fellow of All Souls College Oxford 1921-28, worked in the Home Civil Service 1922-28, then was successively leader writer of the *Daily Mail* 1928-31, *The Times* 1932-61 and *The Daily Telegraph* 1961-67. From 1953 he was Arundel Herald Extraordinary, a position revived for him to reward his historical work on the monarchy and his help with Buckle's history of *The Times* at a time when it was a convention that *Times*' staff should not accept awards in the honours list. WW DNB CA

75 Boy Scouts. E.E. Reynolds
Social Life and Character. 4 cp, 4 sp, 30 bw.
Pub 1944. TLS 30 December. 2nd imp 1944, 3rd revised 1946, in which a picture of Lord Rowallan, Chief Scout, replaced the picture of Lord Somers shown in the other editions.
E 40,181, S 40,598, U oversold.

E. E. (Josh) Reynolds, schoolmaster, scout and writer, b 1904, d October 1980. Taught at the Mathematical School Rochester and The Royal Grammar School Colchester before becoming in 1929 Deputy to the Camp Chief of Gilwell Park, a training establishment for Scouts. In 1934 he retired to devote himself to writing and in 1939 became acting editor of *The Scouter*. At the end of the war he was secretary to Lord Somers' Commission on Scouting. He wrote a biography of Lord Baden-Powell, the founder of the Scout movement, and a number of other books on Scouting. In his last years he began to write books allied to the Roman Catholic faith to which he converted after a lifetime as a Quaker.

76 British Portrait Painters. John Russell
Art and Craftsmanship. 8 cp, 17 bw.
Pub 1944. TLS 10 February 1945.
Included in OV, *Aspects of British Art* (138)
E 14,654, S 14,547, U 107.

John Russell CBE, art critic, b 1919, ed St Paul's School and Magdalen College Oxford. Hon Attache Tate Gallery 1940-41, Ministry of Information 1941-43, naval intelligence 1943-46, regular contributor to *The Sunday Times* from 1945 and its art critic 1949-74. He became art critic of *The New York Times* in 1974 and was its chief art critic from 1982-90. His books include *Seurat* 1965, *Henry Moore* 1968, *Ben Nicholson* 1969, *The World of Matisse* 1970, *Edouard Vuillard* 1971, *Francis Bacon* 1971, and *The Meanings of Modern Art* 1981. WW CA

77 English Pottery and China. Cecilia Sempill
Art and Craftsmanship 8 cp, 29 bw, 1 v.
Pub 1944. TLS 23 June 1945. 2nd imp revised 1945, 3rd 1947. The 2nd imp was re-titled *English Pottery and Porcelain* and contains several changes in the illustrations, both colour and black-and-white. In addition, the flowered tea pot on four legs which adorns the upper dust-jacket and cover of the 1944 edition is replaced in the 1945 and subsequent editions by a much more severe striped teapot without a single leg. Reprinted in 1987 by Bracken Books.
Included in OV, *British Craftsmanship* (139).
E 40,082, S 39,512, U 570.

Lady Cecilia Alice Sempill, sculptor and designer, b 1907, d 19 December 1984, ed Royal College of Art where she won the travelling scholarship for sculpture in 1927. In the late 1930s she founded, with Athol Hay the registrar of the college, the firm of Dunbar-Hay to sell furniture, textiles, pottery and china, much of it commissioned from contemporary designers and artists. The fine works included the only furniture designed by Eric Ravilious, a set of dining room chairs. The war killed the business. In 1941 she married Lord Sempill and after his death in 1965 one of her main occupations was to maintain and restore the Sempill family house, Craigievar Castle, Aberdeenshire, now owned by the Scottish National Trust.

78 Battlefields in Britain. C. V. Wedgwood
History and Achievement. 8 cp, 21 bw.
Pub 1944. TLS 3 February 1945.
E 15,755, S 15,556, U 199.

Dame Cicely Veronica Wedgwood OM, historian, b 20 July 1910, ed Lady Margaret Hall Oxford. Won the James Tait Black prize in 1944 for her history of William the Silent. Probably best known for her books on the seventeenth century, including *The King's Peace* 1955, *The King's War* 1958 and *The Trial of Charles I* 1964, all pub Collins. In 1946 she translated *Auto da Fe* by Elias Canetti. Her superb BP volume is described in Part 1 pp 15-16. WW CA

79 British Botanists. John Gilmour
Natural History. 8 cp, 19 bw.
Pub 1944. TLS 31 March 1945. 2nd imp 1946.
E 29,207, S 20,730, U 8,477, R 8,487

John Scott Lennox Gilmour, botanical scholar, b 28 September 1906 d 3 June 1986, ed Uppingham School and Clare College Cambridge. Curator of the Herbarium and Botanical Museum Cambridge 1930-31, Assistant Director of the Royal Botanic Gardens at Kew 1931-46, worked at the Ministry of Fuel and Power during the war. From 1947-51 Director of the Royal Horticultural Society's Gardens at Wisley and from 1951-73 Director of the University Botanic Gardens Cambridge. His botanical publications were many, including the classic *Wild Flowers of the Chalk* in 1947. From 1943 he was assistant editor of the *New Naturalist* series. WW

80 The English Ballet. W. J. Turner
Art and Craftsmanship 4 cp, 19 bw, 4 ph.
Pub 1944. TLS 28 April 1945. 2nd imp 1946. Reprinted for FOB.
E 58,150, S 55,975, U 3,075 (these figures do not add up, but that is how they appear in the schedule).

The startling account he quotes of the escape of the Sadler's Wells Ballet Company from Holland whilst that country was being invaded by Germany is referred to in Part 1 p 13. See also entries 3 and 133-139.

81 English Letter Writers. C. E. Vulliamy
Literature and Belles Lettres. 8 cp, 24 bw.
Pub 1945. TLS 11 August. 2nd imp 1946.
E 30,217, S 22,358, U 7,859, R 7,690.

Colwyn Edward Vulliamy, scholar, wit and biographer, b 20 June 1886, d 4 September 1971, ed privately. Studied art at Newlyn 1910-13, served in France, Macedonia and Turkey 1914-18, contributed to *The Spectator* and other journals and wrote many books including biographies of Mrs Delaney, Mrs Thrale, James Boswell, George III, Voltaire, Rousseau, and John Wesley. WW CA

82 The Guilds of the City of London. Sir Ernest Pooley
History and Achievement 8 cp, 19 bw.
Pub 1945. TLS 7 July.
E 25,438, S 18,232, U 7,206, R 6,803.

Sir Ernest Henry Pooley, GCVO, administrator, b 20 November 1876, d 13 February

1966, ed Worcester and Pembroke Colleges Oxford. Called to the Bar 1901, Legal Assistant to the Board of Education 1903-05, Assistant Clerk to the Drapers' Company 1905-08, Clerk 1908-44, war service 1914-18 Royal Naval Volunteer Reserve and Royal Garrison Artillery in France and Gallipoli, Master 1944-45, Warden 1952-53 and again in 1962-63. Chairman of the Arts Council 1946-53 and thus saw it through its first seven years, stepping in when the first Chairman, Lord Keynes, died soon after his appointment. He was criticised on appointment to this post for lack of knowledge of the Arts, but exhibited the mixture of common sense and courage which were the prime requirements needed in that thankless task. WW DNB

83 British Railways. Arthur Elton
Science, Medicine and Engineering. 8 cp, 31 bw (not 32 as stated on title page. The total of 31 is obtained by counting as four the illustrations on page 19.)
Pub 1945. O 3 March TLS 8 June 1946. 2nd imp revised 1947.
E 25,284, S 20,292, U 4,992, R 5,072.

Sir Arthur Hallam Rice Elton, tenth baronet, documentary film producer, b 10 February 1906 d 1 January 1973, ed Marlborough School and Jesus College Cambridge. He would escape from Marlborough in company with John Betjeman to haunt the Great Western Railway yards at Swindon and buy the first items of his great collection of books and machinery related to railways. Became a scriptwriter for Gainsborough pictures in 1927 and was one of the group which created the British documentary film movement. He moved easily from his privileged landowning background to the factories and slums of the depression where he pioneered the use of direct film interviews on location. During the 1939-45 war he worked in the Ministry of Information producing many impressive propaganda films. He became an adviser to the Shell company in 1947 and from 1957 was Head of Shell Films, afterwards working on British Transport Films. His collection of prints, books and other objects relating to industrial development in Britain was passed to the Ironbridge Museum in Shropshire on his death. WW DNB

84 English Rivers and Canals. Frank Eyre and Charles Hadfield
Topographical History. 8 cp, 19 bw.
Pub 1945. O 3, TLS 30 March 1946. This first edition, as pointed out in Part 1 p 35, was in fact published in March 1946. 2nd imp 1947.
E 25,273, S 18,462, U 6,811, R 7,512.

Frank Eyre, poet and publisher, b 1910 d 1991. He wrote most of the BP volume. His co-author, Charles Hadfield who researched the book with him and also shared with him fire-fighting duties in London during the war, remembers him as a poet, a racing driver on the Brooklands circuit and a white water canoeist. Frank Eyre went to Australia in 1948 to take charge of the Oxford University Press in that country and never returned to Britain. Another of his books is *The Quiet Spirit.*

Ellis Charles Raymond Hadfield, publisher, water manager and writer, b 5 August 1909, ed Blundell's School and St Edmund Hall Oxford. Worked with Oxford University Press in 1936, Director of Publications with the Central Office of Information 1946-48 and their Controller (Overseas) 1948-62, became Director of David and Charles Publishers 1960-64 (he was the 'Charles'), and was Manager of the British Waterways Board 1962-

66. Has written many books on canals, including the standard work *British Canals* 1950 which has run to many editions. He researched the BP volume with Frank Eyre, contributing in particular the section on canals. He also contributed from his collection of canal artifacts the cover design which is taken from a canal token. He still retains the correspondence with Walter Turner and Sheila Shannon relating to his BP volume and kindly gave me copies to use in the history and the catalogue. WW

85   Islands Round Britain. R. M. Lockley
Topographical History. 8 cp, 27 bw.
Pub 1945. TLS 4 August. 2nd imp 1946.
E 29,492, S 26,048, U 3,444, R 3,034.

Ronald Mathias Lockley, author, farmer, ornithologist, b 8 November 1903. Author of *I Know an Island* and many other books on islands, birds, whales, Wales and New Zealand, where he now lives, aged 90, and is, as he wrote to me '... quite retired at this pleasant Bay of Plenty home where my daughter, born on Skokholm, has an orchard and comes to see me almost daily.' He added that he had had two more books published since his last entry in *Who's Who* in 1992 and that his most successful book was *Britain In Colour* for Batsford which sold about 30,000 copies. WW CA

86   British Journalists and Newspapers. Derek Hudson
Literature and Belles Lettres. 8 cp, 26 bw, including 1 ph.
Pub 1945. TLS 21 July.
E 15,227, S 15,190, U 37.

Derek Rommel Hudson, journalist and author, b 20 July 1911. ('My full name will astonish you,' wrote Derek Hudson to me on 22 September 1993, 'whether the Rommel bears any relationship to the German general, I never discovered. My maternal grandparents were Germans who settled in England circa 1880 and were naturalised. My grandfather was a splendid man, a wool broker. My grandmother a Kerner, of the family of Justinus Kerner, the poet of Weinsberg, still strongly remembered there and in Wurttenberg generally.') Ed Shrewsbury School and Merton College Oxford. After a short period on *The Birmingham Post* joined *The Times* in 1939 and remained on its editorial staff until 1949 having been exempted from military service on health grounds. From 1949-53 Literary Editor of *The Spectator* and from 1955-65 an Editor for the Oxford University Press. He is a prolific author and his books include a biography of Thomas Barnes, Editor of *The Times 1817-41*. In another letter to me of 10 September 1993 he described how his BP volume came about; 'I suggested to my senior colleague W. F. Casey, a charming man who later became Editor, that I might be able to write the book on journalists for the Britain in Pictures series. He knew the editor W. J. Turner well and kindly proposed the idea to him. The result you know.' WW CA

87   Sporting Pictures of England. Guy Paget
Art and Craftsmanship. 12 cp, 21 bw.
Pub 1945. TLS 5 January 1946. Reprinted in 1987 by Bracken Books.
Included in OV, *Aspects of British Art* (138).
E 41,055, S 27,422, U 13,633, R 11,239.

Major Thomas Guy Frederick Paget, landed-gentleman, author, collector, b 1887, d 12 March 1952, ed Eton School. On leaving school, he began immediately to carry out his landlord responsibilities because he had been only 8 years old when his father died. Fought in the 1914-18 war with the 7th Battalion Northamptonshire Regiment serving in France, and also in the Middle-East about which he wrote in his *Chronicle of the Last Crusade*. After the war he continued the life of a landed gentleman, looking after estates in Leicestershire and Nottinghamshire as well as being a Justice of the Peace, Deputy Lieutenant of the County and High Sherriff of Nottinghamshire, and, for one year, Member of Parliament for Bosworth. He served also in the second war in the RAF volunteer reserve, accepting a lower rank than Major in order to get an active job despite his age. He inherited a notable collection of sporting pictures to which he added, becoming a considerable authority. He also wrote many books on hunting, county history and war as well as several biographies. He died after a fall whilst hunting. WW

88 English Watercolour Painters. H.J. Paris
Art and Craftsmanship. 8 cp, 21 bw.
Pub 1945. TLS 29, September. Reprinted in 1987 by Bracken Books.
Included in OV, *Aspects of British Art* (138).
E 18,043, S 17,825, U 218.

Henry John Paris, Gallery Director, b 2 May 1912, d 14 June 1985, ed Brighton College, Brighton College of Art and Worcester College Oxford. He was Deputy Director, Walker Art Gallery Liverpool 1938-39, commissioned in the Royal Artillery 1940, Director National Gallery of South Africa 1949-62 and Director of the National Army Museum 1967-69. WW

89 British Furniture Makers. John Gloag
Art and Craftsmanship. 8 cp, 25 bw.
Pub 1945. TLS 9 June, O 1 July. 2nd imp 1946.
Included in OV, *British Craftsmanship* (139).
E 29,599, S 29,078, U 481, R 257.

John Edwards Gloag, writer, b 10 August 1896, d 17 July 1981, ed Battersea Grammar School, Regent Street Polytechnic and the studio of Thornton-Smith. Served in first war from 1916-18 when he was invalided out and was then successively Technical Editor, Art Editor and Editor of *The Cabinet Maker* until 1927. He wrote over 30 books, twenty five of them novels, and several on furniture and design including *English Furniture* which remained in print for more than forty years and is still regarded as a classic. From 1943-47 he was a member of the Board of Trade Utility Furniture Advisory Committee and was a founder member of the Council of Industrial Design. For a time he was the Question Master on the Brains Trust on BBC radio. CA

90 English Public Schools. Rex Warner
Education and Religion 8 cp, 30 bw.
Pub 1945. O 10 June, TLS 7 July. 2nd imp 1946.
E 33,218, S 26,582, U 6,636, R 5,935.

Rex Warner, University lecturer and writer, b 9 March 1905, d 24 June 1986, ed St

George's School Harpenden and Wadham College Oxford. Schoolmaster in England and Egypt, Director of the British Institute Athens 1945-47, Talman Professor at Bowdoin College 1962-63, and a Professor at the University of Connecticut 1964-74. He wrote many books of poetry and several novels, but will probably be remembered most for his translations of the classics, in particular *The Medea* of Euripides, and for such popular writings on classical mythology as *Men and Gods* 1950. WW

91 Trees in Britain. Alexander L. Howard
Natural History. 8 cp, 18 bw.
Pub 1946. TLS 29 June. Author styled A. L. Howard on spine and Alexander L. Howard on title page.
Included in OV, *Nature in Britain* (136).
E 14,407, S 14,306, U 101.

Alexander L. Howard, d 5 June 1946. He wrote *Manual of the Timbers of the World, Their Characteristics and Uses* in 1920 which was revised in 1934, and contributed several articles on forestry to *Nature*, otherwise nothing known.

92 Early Britain. Jacquetta Hawkes
History and Achievement. 8 cp, 26 bw.
Pub 1945. O 14 October, TLS 10 November. 2nd imp 1946. Reprinted for FOB. Reprinted in 1987 by Bracken Books.
E 33,074, S 27,115, U 5,959, R 1,617.

Jacquetta Hawkes OBE (Mrs J. B. Priestley), author and archaeologist, b 5 August 1910, ed Perse School and Newnham College Cambridge. Carried out research and excavations 1931-40, worked in the Post-War Reconstruction Secretariat 1941-43 and the UK National Commission for UNESCO 1943-49, after which retired from public service to write. Her classic work on *Prehistoric Britain*, written with Christopher Hawkes, had been published in 1944 and her BP volume followed soon after in 1945. WW CA

93 English Cricket. Neville Cardus
Country Life and Sport. 8 cp, 21 bw, including 7 ph.
Pub 1945. TLS 8 December. 2nd imp 1946, 3rd 1947. Reprinted for FOB.
E 63,684, S 40,427, U 23,257, R 10,511.

Sir Neville Cardus CBE, music critic and writer on cricket, b 2 April 1889, d 28 February 1975, ed in Manchester and abroad. He started what was ultimately to become his long association with *The Manchester Guardian* in 1916 as an assistant to the editor C. P. Scott, but was sacked after a month when Scott decided that he needed no help. After a short period as secretary to the Head of Shrewsbury school he rejoined *The Manchester Guardian* as an assistant to the music critic and contributed his first article on cricket in 1919. Thereafter he wrote on both music and cricket until 1940, then joined the *Sydney Morning Herald* until 1947 and returned to England with *The Sunday Times* until he rejoined *The Manchester Guardian* in 1951. A profile of him in *Picture Post* on 12 July 1952 lauded the 'magic' he had brought to writing about cricket '... which became in his prose part of the deathless pageant of the English scene ... the players were raised to the power of a Shakespearian cast.' His report of Tom Richardson bowling himself to a standstill

The Books

had, according to James Agate, a poetic licence unjustified by a prosaically precise memory of the occasion; 'what of that', said *Picture Post*, 'it lives in literature beside Hazlitt's account of the fight between Bill Neate and the Gasman'. Reading his lyrical BP volume one can well believe the anecdote that Neville Cardus as a reporter took time off from a game at Old Trafford to be married, and returned immediately to the ground to note that Makepeace and Hallows had added 17 runs in his absence. WW DNB CA

94 Insect Life in Britain. Geoffrey Taylor
Natural History. 8 cp, 18 bw, 4 v.
Pub 1945. TLS 29 September. 2nd imp 1946.
Included in OV, *Nature in Britain* (136).
E 34,571, S 21,095, U 13,481, R 7,425.

Geoffrey Basil Taylor (born Phibbs), poet and garden historian, b 1900, d 1956. According to Martin Seymour-Smith's *Life of Robert Graves* (pub Hutchinson 1982), Phibbs was described by his friend, the writer Frank O'Connor, as demonic, satanic and cruel, but with an animal beauty. He became embroiled with the household of Robert Graves, becoming, first, Laura Riding's 'Irish Adonis', and then the lover of Graves' wife Nancy, precipitating Riding's suicide attempt in 1929. He taught English in Cairo for a time after 1929. Was disinherited by his father, who refused to receive his mistress, on which changed his surname from Phibbs to his Mother's maiden name of Taylor. His publications include, *Some Nineteenth Century Gardens* 1951, *Victorian Flower Gardens* 1952, and *English Love Poems* prepared with John Betjeman and published after his death in 1957. According to Sheila Shannon he was recommended to Walter Turner as author of this BIP volume by Geoffrey Grigson.

95 English Printed Books. Francis Meynell
Art and Craftsmanship. 8 cp, 21 bw.
Pub 1946. TLS 19 October. Advertised sometimes as *English Books*.
E 30,180, S 20,867, U 9,313, R 8,888.

Sir Francis George Meynell, typographer and book producer, b 12 May 1891, d 9 July 1975, ed St Anthony's School Eastbourne, Downside School and Trinity College Dublin which he left without a degree. He worked for a period with his father, Wilfred Meynell a director of the publisher's Burns Oates, founded the Pelican Press in 1916, became a director of *The Daily Herald* 1918-20, founded the Nonesuch Press in 1923, was typographic adviser to the Stationery Office 1945-66 when he was responsible for much of the official printing for the Festival of Britain in 1951 and the Coronation in 1952, and was Director General of the Cement and Concrete Association 1946-58. WW DNB CA

96 British Dogs. A. Croxton Smith
Country Life and Sport. 8 cp, 24 bw.
Pub 1945. No review in O or TLS. 2nd imp 1946.
E 45,962, S 34,694, U 11,268, R 8,594.

Arthur Croxton Smith OBE, writer and dog breeder, b 3 December 1865, d 27 August 1952, ed privately. Articled at *The Northampton and Daily Reporter*, Assistant Editor of *Gentlewoman* which he left in 1909 in order to concentrate on his own writing and also to develop his interest in dogs. In the war of 1914-18 was Director of Publicity at the Ministry of Food and subsequently served on Government committees during emergencies such as coal and railway strikes and the General Strike of 1926. Wrote many books and articles about dogs, including Tail-Wagger chats under the pseudonym 'Philoknon'. As Hon Sec of the Association of Bloodhound Breeders he organised manhunting trials and was one of the first to encourage the use of dogs in police work. His BP volume was published when he was 80 years of age. WW

97 British Weather. Stephen Bone
Science, Medicine and Engineering. 8 cp, 29 bw.
Pub 1946. TLS 28 September.
E 14,488, S 14,517, U oversold.

Stephen Bone, landscape and portrait painter, b 13 November 1904, d 15 September 1958, ed Bedales School and Slade School of Art. Apart from a period as London Art Critic of *The Manchester Guardian* and occasional broadcasts, he lived by his art. As early as 1925 he won the Gold Medal at the Paris Exhibition for wood engravings, and later painted murals for the underground railway, but main achievements were in landscape painting, especially in oils. He loved to travel and one of the biggest exhibitions of his work was in Sweden in 1937. During the war of 1939-45 was an official war artist in the Navy. His paintings are exhibited in many British galleries, including the Tate. He was an inspired choice for the BP volume on *British Weather* because in addition to art his main interests were geography and writing, and his BP book made wonderful use of his gifts in all three. The illustrations are among the best in the series. In a series about Britain it would have been a terrible failure to write a dull book about the British weather, and Stephen Bone does not fail. WW DNB

98 English Hymns and Hymn Writers. Adam Fox
Education and Religion. 8 cp, 22 bw.
Pub 1947. No review in O or TLS.
E 17,892, S 11,758, U 6,034, R 5,143.

Canon Adam Fox, priest, schoolmaster and poet, b 15 July 1883, d 17 January 1977, ed Winchester College and University College Oxford. Ordained in 1913 whilst still an assistant master at Lancing College. From 1918-24 Warden of Radley College and in 1925 became an assistant master at the Diocesan College, South Africa. Fellow and Dean of Magdalen College Oxford from 1929-42, Oxford's Professor of Poetry 1938-42, and Canon of Chichester Cathedral 1936-42. He wrote mainly on religious and philosophical themes, including *Plato for Pleasure*, and also poetry including the long poem *Old King Coel*. In his brief biography in *Contemporary Authors* he says that 'I am called Adam because I had a twin sister called Eve. I am an amateur author. I do not earn my living by my writings, and I try to persuade myself that I shall best please the public by first pleasing myself.' WW CA

99 English Glass. W. B. Honey
Art and Craftsmanship. 8 cp, 26 bw.
Pub 1946. TLS 4 January 1947. Reprinted for FOB. Reprinted in 1987 by Bracken Books.

Included in OV, *British Craftsmanship* (139).
E 26,230, S 21,062, U 5,168.

William Bowyer Honey CBE, museum curator, b 13 April 1889, d 13 September 1956, ed Sir Walter St John's School Battersea. Keeper of Department of Ceramics at the Victoria and Albert Museum 1938-50. Wrote many books about glass and porcelain, including the V & A Handbook 1946, *Guide to Later Chinese Porcelain* 1927, *Old English Porcelain* 1928, *English Pottery and Porcelain* 1933 and an *Historical Survey and Dictionary of Ceramic Art*, Volume 1 in 1949 and Volume 2 in 1952. WW

100 The English People. George Orwell
Social Life and Character. 8 cp, 17 bw.
Pub 1947. O 3, TLS 23 August. Reprinted for FOB.
E 23,118, S 18,275, U 4,843, R 316. Advertised first as *The British People* to be written by George Orwell or Edmund Blunden or Sir John Squire.

George Orwell, pseudonym for Eric Arthur Blair, writer, b 25 June 1903, d 21 January 1950, ed Eton. Apart from five years in the Burma Police and some years as a schoolmaster, tramp and dishwasher, his main work was writing. Before his BIP book he had written *Burmese Days* 1934, *The Road to Wigan Pier* 1937, *Homage to Catalonia* 1938, *Coming up for Air* 1939, *Animal Farm* 1945 and *Critical Essays* 1946. *Nineteen Eighty Four* came later in 1949. WW DNB CA

101 Life Among the Scots. Janet Adam Smith
Social Life and Character. 8 cp, 21 bw.
Pub 1946. TLS 15 February 1947.
E 26,220, S 21,316, U 4,904, R 5,387. (See also entry 126.)

Janet Buchanan Adam Smith OBE (Mrs John Carleton), author and journalist, b 9 December 1905, ed Cheltenham Ladies College and Somerville College Oxford. BBC 1928-35, was Assistant Editor of *The Listener* 1930-35, Assistant Literary Editor of the *New Statesman and Nation* 1949-52 and its Literary Editor 1952-60. Her publications include a number of books on Robert Louis Stevenson, *The Faber Book of Children's Verse* 1953, *Collected Poems of Michael Roberts* (who was her first husband until his death in a climbing accident) and two books on John Buchan — a biography in 1965 and *John Buchan and his World* in 1979. WW CA

102 English Popular and Traditional Art. Enid Marx and Margaret Lambert
Art and Craftsmanship. 8 cp, 29 bw (not 30 as stated on title page). Order of authors as shown on the title page; on dust-jacket and cover order is reversed, showing Margaret Lambert first.
Pub 1946. No review in O or TLS. Reprinted for FOB.
Included in OV, *British Craftsmanship* (139).
E 26,977, S 18,612, U 8,365, R 5,009.

Enid Crystal Dorothy Marx, artist, b 20 October 1902, ed Roedean School, the Central School of Arts and Crafts and the Royal College of Art Painting School. 1925-39 designed and hand-printed textiles, some of which were bought by the Victoria and Albert museum. Member of the Board of Trade Design Panel on utility furniture. One of the original members of the National Register of Industrial Designers. Designed the postage stamps for the first issue of the reign of Queen Elizabeth II. In addition to illustrating many children's books wrote, again with Margaret Lambert, *English Popular Art* 1952. WW

The Honourable Margaret Barbara Lambert CMG, historian, b 7 November 1906, ed Lady Margaret Hall Oxford. Worked for the European Service of the BBC 1939-45, Assistant Editor of *British Documents on Foreign Policy* 1946-50 (and between 1951-83 remained Editor-in-Chief of German Foreign Office Documents), Lecturer in Modern European History at the University College of the South West 1950-51 and at St Andrew's University 1956-60. In addition to publications with Enid Marx on popular art, published in 1934 *The Saar* and, in 1937, *When Victoria Began To Reign.* WW

103 British Garden Flowers. George M. Taylor
Country Life and Sport. 8 cp, 27 bw (not 26 as stated on tp).
Pub 1946. TLS 29 June. 2nd imp 1947.
E 32,756, S 23,240, U 9,516, R 5,714. (See also entry 108.)

George M. Taylor, gardener, b 1875, d 1 January 1955. Neither the dust-jacket of his BP volume nor his obituary in *The Gardener's Chronicle* provide many biographical details. He was obviously an eminent horticulturalist, honoured by The Royal Horticultural Society and The Royal Caledonian Horticultural Society. Wrote many books on horticulture, including *Roses, Their Culture and Management, The Book of the Rose, Lilies For Beginners,* and *The Little Garden* which was very popular in both Britain and the United States of America where he had a large following. Especially interested in amateur groups of gardeners such as the Paisley weavers with their skill in growing and breeding auriculas, pinks and tulips.

104 British Ships and Shipbuilders. George Blake
Science, Medicine and Engineering. 8 cp, 29 bw.
Pub 1946. TLS 16 November.
E 21,302, S 17,167, U 4,135, R 4,097.

George Blake, novelist and broadcaster, b 28 October 1893, d 29 August 1961, ed Greenock Academy. Became an articled clerk until 1914-18 war in which he was badly wounded. Afterwards resumed law, but soon took up writing, starting as a book reviewer for *Glasgow Herald.* Then acting editor of *John O' London's Weekly* 1924-28, Editor of *The Strand Magazine* 1928-30, and a Director of Faber and Faber 1930-32. By 1946, the year of his BP volume, he had published 18 novels, most of them about Clydeside. In 1960, just before his death, he published a *History of Lloyd's Register of Shipping.* WW

105 British Drawings. Michael Ayrton
Art and Craftsmanship. 8 cp, 25 bw. Line drawing by Mathew Paris reproduced on the front dust-jacket and cover (one of three departures from usual cover design, others being 25 and 34).
Pub 1946. No review in O or TLS.
Included in OV, *Aspects of British Art* (138).
E 22,074, S 16,013, U 6,061, R 5,958.

Michael Ayrton, (born with the surname Gould which he changed in favour of his mother's maiden surname when he became a practising artist), painter, sculptor, author, designer, b 20 February 1921, d 17 November 1975, ed art schools in London, and in Vienna and Paris. Saw the siege of Barcelona during the Spanish civil war and was later invalided out of the RAF. Like John Piper, worked in many art and other mediums, including broadcasting, television and film making, but never enjoyed Piper's fame and public honour. His DNB biographer wrote that '... in a country and society which still regards amateurism as a professional advantage, Ayrton suffered from his relentless curiosity, his considerable eclecticism, and his formidable erudition, backed by a strong physical presence which many people of weaker intellect or personality found intimidating.' When designing the set for John Gielgud's production of *Macbeth* he was rebuked by Gielgud for his '... ungraciousness of manner ... towards the work people in every department'; and (Sir) Kenneth Clark turned him down as a war artist because his specimen paintings were thought to be too grimly unpatriotic. Henry Moore described him as '... a significant eccentric'. In 1994 his step-granddaughter wrote his biography and *The Sunday Times* review by Waldemar Januszczak acknowledged his proficiency, but suggested that he failed to achieve anything really memorable, dismissing him as a talker and networker. *The Times* reviewer Derwent May on the other hand considered that this biography might prove to be the first step in a much needed revival of appreciation of Ayrton's work. Obviously, nearly twenty years after his death he remains as controversial as ever, and the fierce strength of his BP volume helps one to understand why. WW DNB CA

106 English Essayists. Bonamy Dobrée
Literature and Belles Lettres. 8 cp, 23 bw.
Pub 1946. TLS 29 March 1947.
E 23,108, S 15,935, U 7,173, R 7,087.

Lt Col Professor Bonamy Dobrée, teacher and writer, b 2 February 1891, d 3 September 1974, ed Haileybury School, Royal Military Academy Woolwich and, after 1914-18 war, Cambridge. Commissioned in the army in 1910, resigned in 1913 and re-joined for the war. Lecturer in the East London College 1925-26, Professor of English at the Egyptian University Cairo 1926-29, and a writer and journalist 1929-35. Served in the second war 1939-45. Publications include many biographies, ranging from John Wesley to Giacomo Casanova, and Milton to Ouida, as well as many books on poetry and English literature generally. His DNB biographer writes that 'Like Swift he enjoyed the bagatelle, and like him he enjoyed it in good company. His many friends included T.S. Eliot, Virginia Woolf, Wyndham Lewis and Henry Moore. He was also a soldier. His military training had given him a briskness that enabled him to execute his business, whether teaching, writing, or administration, with prompt efficiency. This left him time for the civilities of life ...' WW DNB CA

107 British Golf. Bernard Darwin
Country Life and Sport, 8 cp, 27 bw (including 15 ph).
Pub 1946. No review in O or TLS.
E 23,098, S 17,174, U 5,924, R 7,964. See also entry 63.

Bernard Richard Meirion Darwin CBE, whose biographical details other than those which relate to golf are in entry 63. His writings on Clubs and clubs are both attractive, but his volume on golf combines grace with authority and matches the Cardus volume on cricket (93). He was Golf Correspondent for *The Times* for 39 years and wrote regularly also for *Country Life*. He played golf for Cambridge, being Captain in 1897, and for England on eight occasions, on one of which he took over as Captain when the appointed Captain fell ill. When he began to write, golf reporting was scanty, but by his retirement, according to the DNB, he had '... turned it into a branch of literary journalism.' WW DNB

108 British Herbs and Vegetables. George M. Taylor
Country Life and Sport. 8 cp, 27 bw.
Pub 1947. No review in O or TLS.
E 18,356, S 13,816, U 4,540, R 5,047. See also entry 103.

109 British Anglers' Natural History. E. G. Boulenger
Natural History. 8 cp, 22 bw.
Pub 1946. TLS 26 April 1947.
E 18,300, S 10,802, U 7,498, R 2,754.

Edward George Boulenger, curator, b 8 May 1888, d 30 April 1946, ed St Paul's School. Curator of Reptiles and Lower Vertebrates at the Zoological Society 1911-23 (during the first world war he acted as a balloon observer) and Director of the Society's Aquarium 1923-43, resuming his earlier responsibilities in addition from 1937-43. Served on the General Staff of the War Office during the second war. Publications mainly on reptiles and fish, but include works on apes and monkeys. WW

110 British Universities. S. C. Roberts
Education and Religion. 8 cp, 23 bw.
Pub 1947. TLS 6 December.
E 22,819, S 13,284, U 9,565, R 8,395.

Sir Sydney Castle Roberts, university teacher, b 3 April 1887, d 21 July 1966, ed Brighton College and Pembroke College Cambridge. Assistant Secretary of the Cambridge University Press 1911-14, wounded in the 1914-18 war, then Secretary of the Press 1922-48 and Master of Pembroke College Cambridge 1948-58. During this last period he was also Vice Chancellor of the University 1949-51, Vice President of the International Association of Universities 1950-55 and Chairman of the British Film Institute 1952-56. Sir Sydney was a great 'Johnsonian' and wrote several books about the great man as well as presiding over the Johnson Society in 1929. He also wrote an illustrated British history, a *History of the Cambridge University Press* 1921, books on Sherlock Holmes and Dr Watson and a sequel to Max Beerbohm's Zuleika Dobson, *Zuleika in Cambridge*. WW

111 British Clocks and Clockmakers. Kenneth Ullyett
Art and Craftsmanship. 8 cp, 24 bw.
Pub 1947. No review in O or TLS. Reprinted in 1987 by Bracken Books.
Included in OV, *British Craftsmanship* (139).
E 17,979, S 14,985, U 2,994, R 1,920.

The Books 111

Kenneth Ullyett is described on the dust-jacket as a noted collector of antique clocks and watches. He was also a vintage car collector and restorer. In the 1960s he edited a series of books about cars published by Max Parrish. His book on *Watch Collecting* was published for the first time in 1970 by Frederick Muller and he referred in it to his BP volume. The only other information I have gleaned is that he was a magistrate, hereditary Lord of the Manor of Hanworth, Middlesex, and died in a car crash.

112 The English at the Seaside. Christopher Marsden
Social Life and Character. 8 cp, 25 bw.
Pub 1947. TLS 16 August.
E 22,999, S 11,312, U 11,687, R 5,698.

Christopher Marsden, writer and radio producer, b 10 March 1912, d 24 December 1989, ed Westminster School and University College Oxford. He was Literary Editor of *The Geographical Magazine*, served with the artillery during the 1939-45 war and then from 1946-70 worked for the BBC world service as a talks producer. He wrote a study of the first days of St Petersburg *Palmyra of the North* which was published when that city, then known as Leningrad, was being attacked by German troops and was reviewed as '... extraordinarily well written, discerning and enjoyable'. In 1953 he wrote the volume on *Nottinghamshire* in the County Books series, again very well reviewed as employing '... a colloquial style of great charm'. His only other published work was his BP volume, which in style and enjoyment lives up to his other books. When stationed on the South Coast 1940-42 he began to accumulate material about the seaside and rarely can time have been better spent.

113 Roman Britain. Ian Richmond
History and Achievement. 8 cp, 22 bw.
Pub 1947. No review in O or TLS. Reprinted for FOB. Reprinted in 1987 by Bracken Books.
E 21,677, S 14,022, U 7,655, R 4,202.

Sir Ian Archibald Richmond CBE, historian, b 10 May 1902, d 4 August 1965, ed Ruthin School and Corpus Christi College Oxford. Lecturer at the University of Belfast 1926-30, Director British School Rome 1930-32, Lecturer 1935-43, Reader 1945-50, and Professor of Roman History at the University of Durham at King's College. Most of his historical writing was for historical and archeological journals, but he wrote several books including *City Wall of Imperial Rome* 1930, and *Roman Britain* for the Oxford and Pelican histories 1948 and 1955 respectively. He carried out notable excavations at Hadrian's Wall and elsewhere. His knowledge of Roman Britain was said to have caused his hearers to wonder whether he had not personally witnessed the Roman army at work. WW DNB CA

114 British Yachting. C. St John Ellis
Not published, but planned for BP, Country Life and Sport.

115 The Port of London. John Herbert
Topographical History. 8 cp, 19 bw.
Pub 1947. O 15 February, TLS 27 March 1948.
E 17,052, S 8,683, U 8,369, R 5,921.

John Herbert, journalist and company director, b 24 May 1924, ed Winchester and New College Oxford. Royal Navy 1942-46, journalist 1948-55 successively on *The Glasgow Herald*, the *Daily Mail*, and *The Daily Telegraph*, then public relations with the firm of Patrick Dolan, later taken over by Christie's of whose Board Mr Herbert became a Member and public relations director 1959-85. He wrote *Inside Christie's*, pub by Hodder and Stoughton 1990. He described his work on the BIP volume in a letter to me of 24 August 1994 as follows: 'In 1946 I was returning in the New Zealand Shipping Company's Rimutaka — I'd been dragged off my beloved destroyer and made Flag-Lieut to the Vice-Admiral (Q) British Pacific Fleet — after two years away from UK. We had left Melbourne and were due to berth in the Thames at Tilbury. I radioed my father (APH) and suggested that he brought his Water Gipsy (which had been in the Royal Naval Auxiliary Patrol Service during the war), down to meet me so that I could go the whole way from Melbourne to Hammersmith by water. This he did, accompanied by my mother. As a result of this form of homecoming I wrote a suitably slushy piece and for some crazy reason sent it up to *The Spectator*. I was not surprised to get it back, but with the rejection slip was a letter from Turner, who lived at No 9 then, three doors east of my parents, asking whether I would be interested in writing a history of The Port of London and if so to send a synopsis. Up till then I had had nothing published... So when Turner asked for a synopsis I was as green as green could be from a literary point of view, but evidently they were satisfied as I duly was commissioned to write the book. This was not long before I went up to New College in October 1946, having been demobilised in July. I was meant to be reading PPE, which was ambitious enough, without having to get down to researching the rise of the Port of London, through books borrowed from the London Library by my mother and also from the Port of London Authority's library. I gather Sir John Anderson, later Lord Waverly, was very keen on the BIP's decision to commission a book on the Port. Well it was done as you know; typed on a portable Remington typewriter; much of it in the small hours. I got quite a lot of pleasure seeing it fill the windows of Blackwells, as my father had done the same in his day at Oxford.' APH is Sir Alan Herbert who wrote for *Punch* and who spoke at the luncheon which launched the publication of the first eight volumes of the BIP series (see p 31); Turner is, of course, W. J. Turner, then still literary editor of *The Spectator* and who was to die only four months after commissioning John Herbert's book.

116 British Hills and Mountains. Peter Bicknell
Topographical History. 8 cp, 23 bw.
Pub 1947. O 15 February 1948.
E 15,172, S 8,226, U 6,946, R 3,096.

Peter Bicknell, architect and university lecturer in architecture, b 16 June 1907, ed Oundle School and Jesus College Cambridge. Has a special interest in the art and literature of the hills, having known the hills of Northumberland and the Lake District from childhood and later coming to know the hills and mountains of Wales and Scotland. A committed mountaineer in Britain and the Alps. Was President of the Climbers' Club. During the second world war he took part in experimental courses in North Wales to train army cadets in mountaineering. His architectural commissions include buildings for the National Trust, the Wildfowl Trust and the Scott Polar Research Institute. In addition to his BP volume and other writings in specialist journals, he wrote in 1984 *The Illustrated*

Wordsworth Guide to the Lakes and in 1990 *The Picturesque Scenery of the Lake District: a Bibliographical Study*. Now, in 1994, aged 87, he maintains a lively interest in mountains, scenery and painting and during his retirement has arranged, and written the catalogues for, many exhibitions related to Landscape painting and the Lakes. His letter to me in June 1994 has been referred to in Part 1 pp 33 and 48 with its comments on selecting illustrations for his BP volume. 'It was for me a very happy episode and started me on what after my retirement as an architect was to become almost a second vocation. I found the editing sympathetic and efficient and only disagreed on the policy which you discuss of the relation of illustrations to text ... so I am glad that I was not alone in thinking that a close relationship was essential in a series of Britain *In Pictures*.'

117 The House of Commons. Martin Lindsay MP
History and Achievement. 8 cp, 20 bw.
Pub 1947. TLS 22 November.
E 17,617, S 15,294, U 2,323, R 1,265.

Sir Martin Alexander Lindsay CBE DSO, first baronet of Dowhill, soldier, explorer, politician, author, b 22 August 1905, d 5 May 1981, ed Wellington School (where he won the English essay prize) and The Royal Military Academy Sandhurst. Commissioned in 1925 in the Royal Scots Fusiliers and in 1927 seconded to the Nigeria Regiment, during which period he travelled across Africa through the Ituri Forest in the Belgian Congo accompanied only by porters. He endured considerable hardship, but managed still to collect various artifacts of the Pigmy people for the British Museum. Volunteered for the Greenland expedition 1930-31 and was awarded the King's Polar Medal; wrote about his experiences in *Those Greenland Days* 1932. Arranged his own expedition to the East Coast of Greenland when he sledged 1050 miles in 103 days over the ice cap and mapped 350 miles of mountains; this was described in *Sledge* in 1935. Although elected in 1936 for the Brigg constituency in Lincolnshire he served in Norway during the war when he commanded a battalion of Gordon highlanders in 16 operations and was twice wounded, being awarded the DSO; he wrote a war diary *So Few Got Through* in 1946. In 1945 elected Conservative MP for the Solihull Constituency of Birmingham, a seat he retained until 1964. WW CA

118 British Humour. D. B. Wyndham-Lewis
Not published, but planned for BP, Social Life and Character.

119 The British Theatre. Bernard Miles
Art and Craftsmanship. 8 cp, 21 bw.
Pub 1948. TLS 27 March.
E 15,664, S 13,203, U 2,861.

Baron Miles of Blackfriars CBE, actor and theatre impressario, b 27 September 1907, d 14 June 1991, ed Uxbridge County School and Pembroke College Oxford. First stage appearance as the second messenger in Richard III at the New Theatre in 1930. Thereafter appeared in theatre, music hall, films and on radio. Founded the Mermaid Theatre at Puddle Dock in the City of London in 1959. Wrote several books including *Favourite Tales From Shakespeare* 1976. WW

120 British Windmills and Watermills. C. P. Skilton
Science, Medicine and Engineering. 8 cp, 24 bw.
Pub 1947. No review in O or TLS.
E 15,888, S 9,415, U 6,473, R 4,468.

Charles Skilton, publisher, b 1921, d 1990, ed Alleyns School. First job with Stanley Gibbons then George Allen and Unwin. Imprisoned in 1942 as a conscientious objector. In 1943 began publishing on his own account. His notable, if disparate, successes included the Billy Bunter books and, in the 1960s, a number of erotic classics including John Clelland's *Fanny Hill*. He was active in the windmills and watermills section of the Society for the Protection of Ancient Buildings.

121 English Fashion. Alison Settle
Social Life and Character. 8 cp, 23 bw.
Pub 1948. O 18 July TLS 7 August. Reprinted for FOB
E 16,096, S 14,049, U 2,047, R 196.

Alison Settle OBE, fashion writer, b 1890, d 16 September 1980. Began career at 16 as a secretary and ended it, unwillingly, at 83 when she retired from *The Lady*. In between was a journalist with *The Daily Herald*, wrote two regular columns for ladies in *The Sunday Pictorial*, was Fashion Editor of *Vogue* 1926-33, and then for 22 years Fashion Editor of *The Observer*. Her bustling enthusiasm, bursting handbag and unparalleled experience were legendary. Her obituary in *The Observer* described her as the Miss Marple of fashion journalism '... a sweet, gentle, fuddy-duddy old lady, all lace and fumbling and looking for her glasses, and underneath it all she was shrewd, efficient and extremely knowledgeable. Altering one word of Alison's feature was dangerous work, not lightly undertaken.' She published *Clothes Line* in 1937, *Fashion As A Career* in 1963 and *Paris Fashion* in 1972.
WW

122 The Conservative Party. Nigel Birch
History and Achievement. 50p, 4 cp, 21 bw. As well as being the first volume to extend to 50 pages, this volume is the first also to have only four colour plates, a limitation which was shared by seven of the remaining 11 books in the series.
Pub 1949. TLS 29 July.
E 12,060, S 7,870, U 4,190, R 3,443.

Evelyn Nigel Chetwode Birch, Baron Rhyl, stockbroker and politician, b 18 November 1906, d 8 March 1981, ed Eton. Served in Second War on General Staff and in 1945 was elected as Conservative MP for West Flintshire. In later Conservative Governments was appointed Parliamentary Secretary to the Air Ministry and then to the Ministry of Defence. Appointed Minister of Works in 1954, Secretary of State for Air in 1955, and Economic Secretary to the Treasury in 1957, a post from which he resigned on 6 January 1958 along with Peter Thorneycroft and Enoch Powell. A stern advocate of strictly honest public finance, the subject of his resignation, and an effective debater with a mordant wit. He once described the Treasury as having '... the reckless courage of a mouse at bay'; exclaimed on High Dalton's resignation that '... they've shot our fox'; and at the time of the Profumo scandal called for the Prime Minister's resignation, quoting from Browning's 'The Lost Leader' the words 'Never Glad Confident Morning Again'. WW DNB CA

The Books

123 The Liberal Party. R. J. Cruikshank
History and Achievement. 50 p, 4 cp, 19 bw.
Pub 1948 (this is the date on the title page, but it was almost certainly issued in 1949 with the other two political volumes, the three being reviewed together in July of that year). TLS 29 July 1949.
E 16,256, S 7,113, U 9,143, R 3,190.

Robert James Cruikshank, journalist, b 19 April 1898, d 14 May 1956. Started his newspaper life on *The Bournemouth Guardian* then became in 1919 foreign correspondent of *The Daily News* with which he stayed all his life, including the time when it merged with the *News Chronicle*. From 1928-36 was the paper's representative in New York and in 1941 headed the American Directorate at the Ministry of Information. He was said to have done more than any other journalist to make England and the English known to and understood by Americans. Became Editor of the *News Chronicle* 1947-54 having written a history of the paper in 1946, *Roaring Century*. Other publications included a book on *Charles Dickens and Early Victorian England* 1949. WW DNB

124 The Labour Party. William Glenvil Hall
History and Achievement. 50 p, 4 cp, 22 bw.
Pub 1949. TLS 29 July.
E 12,383, S 6,961, U 5,422, R 3,207

William Glenvil Hall MP, politician, b 4 April 1887, d 13 October 1962, ed Friends' School Saffron Walden. Qualified as a barrister, but worked first in London as a bank clerk, living in Whitechapel where he did social work in the East End. Joined the Independent Labour Party in 1905 and later, although a Quaker, enlisted in the first world war in which he served with The Buffs and then the tank corps, being wounded on one occasion. Became MP for Portsmouth in 1924 but was defeated in 1931 and was out of Parliament until he became MP for Colne Valley in 1939, a seat he held until his death. In the post-war Labour Government was Financial Secretary to the Treasury 1945-50. Very popular MP, people of all parties warming to his attractive personality. At the 1929 election he had been supported by the Marquis of Tavistock who thought he was the sort of man the country needed in Parliament. Something of the flavour of his BP volume on the Labour Party can be gained from his openly expressed regret (page 18) that the works of Karl Marx had not been buried with him in Highgate cemetery. WW DNB

125 British Butterflies. Vere Temple
Natural History. 8 cp, 22 bw.
Pub 1949. TLS 18 November.
E 12,010, S 6,502, U 5,508, R 4,421

Vere Lucy Temple, entomologist, writer and artist, b 8 February 1898 d 198(?), ed Roedean School. Born in the village of Bishopstrow, Wiltshire, the manor of which and its estates had been in the family since 1551. In 1941 she bought 'King's Chase' cottage, reputed to have been used by King John, where she lived for the rest of her life. Fellow of the Royal Entomological Society and wrote mainly about insects, especially butterflies, but also wrote and illustrated *The Observer Book of British Birds* and *The Birds of the Lebanon* under her married name of S. Vere Benson. According to an acquaintance, Dr T.

Lawson, she died in the mid 1980s. He recalls meeting her on a bird-watching trip to Turkey where '... although she was twice my age, she left me standing when climbing hills'. Many of her illustrations of flowers and insects have graced other volumes, and her BP volume on Butterflies includes seven of her own drawings, which is not too many because they are exquisite.

126   Children's Illustrated Books. Janet Adam Smith
Art and Craftsmanship 50 p, 4 cp, 33 bw.
Pub 1948. TLS 12 February, 1949. (This was probably published in 1949, not only because of the review date, but also because the sales figures begin in that year.)
E 14,910, S 9,302, U 5,608, R 1,920. See also entry 101.

127   British Chess. Kenneth Matthews
Social Life and Character. 50 p, 4 cp, 24 bw.
Pub 1948. No review in O or TLS. (Although it appears in sequence with 1949 volumes, the publication date probably was 1948 as there are sales figures for that year.)
E 16,264, S 8,726, U 7,538, R 7,467. See also entry 60.

128   English Cottages and Farmhouses. C. Henry Warren
Country Life and Sport. 8 cp, 27 bw.
Pub 1948. TLS 9 October.
E 15,095, S 10,586, U 4,509, R 4,095. See also entry 46.

Clarence Henry Warren, author and broadcaster, b 12 June 1895, d 3 April 1966, ed Maidstone Grammar School and Goldsmith's College University of London. Schoolmaster 1922-24, a lecturer in the National Portrait Gallery 1927, BBC 1929-33. Wrote a large number of books, mainly about the English countryside, and edited the uniform edition of the works of Richard Jefferies. WW

129   The Turf. John Hislop
Country Life and Sport. 8 cp, 23 bw.
Pub 1948. TLS 26 March 1949. (Probably published in 1949 because no sales are recorded until that year, which is also the year of review, and, as in other 1949 books, the name of W. J. Turner as General Editor no longer appears.)
E15,060, S 9,307, U 5,753, R 5,624.

John Hislop MC, jockey and horse trainer, b 12 December 1911, d 23 February 1994, ed Wellington School and Sandhurst from where he was invalided out after having a kidney removed, a loss which does not seem to have impaired a very active life and subsequent distinguished war service. From 1930 worked at the stables of Victor Gilpin until war service with the Surrey and Sussex Yeomanry in France in 1939-40. Following evacuation from Dunkirk suffered a riding accident at Cheltenham which kept him out of the army for 18 months, after which he served with the 'Phantom' regiment, being parachuted into France and Holland where his bravery earned him the award of the Military Cross. Leading amateur rider on the Flat for 13 years, mainly after the war; and in steeplechasing was third in the Grand National of 1947 riding Kame. General manager of *The British Racehorse* from 1949 and Racing Correspondent for *The Observer* 1946-62 and then for *The News of the World.* Elected to the Jockey Club in 1972, at the time a unique honour for a racing correspondent, but one which recognised his achievements in the saddle, in breeding horses, and in writing about horses and horse racing. Among his many books *Anything But a Soldier* 1965 and *Far From A Gentleman* 1960 were best sellers. Shortly before his death, Mr Hislop gave me a lively and entertaining account of his career, modestly ignoring details such as his Military Cross. He said that he remembered one of the Collins brothers in the SAS during the war being nicknamed 'Brides In The Bath Collins' because of his ingenious, and usually lethal, schemes for bringing the war to an earlier end.

130 British Boxing. Denzil Batchelor
Country Life and Sport. 8 cp, 27 bw including 9 ph.
Pub 1948. TLS 12 June.
E 16,354, S 9,508, U 6,846, R 7,295.

Denzil Stanley Batchelor, author and journalist, b 23 February 1903, d 6 September 1969, ed Trent College Derby and Worcester College Oxford. Began journalism with two Sydney Newspapers, *The Morning Sun* and *The Morning Herald*, until 1937. During the Second World War was in the War Office in London and then became Sports Editor first of *The Leader* magazine and then of *Picture Post* from 1949-57. Was in addition a radio and TV broadcaster and wrote many books on cricket and boxing as well as some thrillers. WW

131 British Hospitals. A. G. L. Ives
Science, Medicine and Engineering. 50 p, 4 cp, 26 bw.
Pub 1948. No review in O or TLS.
E 16,354, S 7,200, U 6,846, R 3,587.

Arthur Glendinning Loveless Ives, administrator, b 19 August 1904, d 1 October 1991, ed Kingswood School and Queen's College Oxford. Started work with the London Chamber of Commerce from 1928-29 then joined King Edward's Hospital Fund for London in 1929 and was Secretary of the Fund from 1938-60. His BP volume was written at a time when the voluntary and public hospitals were coming together under the National Health Service. WW

132 British Farm Stock. The Earl of Portsmouth
Country Life and Sport. 50 p, 4 cp, 33 bw.
Pub 1950. TLS 24 March 1950.
E 5,780, S 2,048, U 3,732, R 3,587

Gerard Vernon Wallop, 9th Earl of Portsmouth, farmer and author, b 16 May 1898, d 28 September 1984. MP for Basingstoke 1929-34 and author of five books, including an autobiography in 1965 *A Knot of Roots*, in addition to his BP volume. There is something appropriate about the fact that the last book in the BIP series, which started with our poets, should be about our animals, for as the author writes, 'The animal blood in the small United Kingdom has been as outstanding as its human blood in its passage across high prairie, bush and forest.' WW

OMNIBUS VOLUMES

133 The British Commonwealth and Empire. W.J. Turner (Editor)
OV 324 pp, 48 cp, 173 bw. Pub 1943. No review in O or TLS. 2nd imp Spring 1945. Introduction by W.J. Turner (see also entries 3, 80, and below). Consists of BC volumes Australia (5); East Africa (6); Canada (9); India (10); South Africa (18); New Zealand (26); and the BP volume The British Colonial Empire (40). It contains the full texts and all the bw illustrations of each of the individual volumes, but only a selection of their colour illustrations.

134 Impressions of English Literature. W.J. Turner (Editor)
OV, 324 pp, 48 cp, 125 bw. Pub 1945. No review in O or TLS. 2nd imp 1945, 3rd 1947. Introduction by Kate O'Brien (see also entry 55). Consists of The English Poets (1); English Novelists (23); British Dramatists (32); British Historians (49); English Diaries And Journals (55); British Philosophers (60); and The English Bible (66). The text of each volume is reproduced complete. All the illustrations are included for the volumes on poets, dramatists, philosophers and the Bible, but the others have lost between 2 and 4 illustrations each. Another edition of this Omnibus Volume was published in 1984 by Thames and Hudson which included volumes 1, 23, 32 and 55, but omitted volumes 49, 60 and 66, and contained an Afterword by Anthony Burgess, and some second thoughts of Lord David Cecil, for which see Part 1 p 61.

135 The Englishman's Country. W.J. Turner (Editor)
OV 319 pp, 48 cp, 137 bw. Published 1945. TLS 13 April 1946. 2nd imp 1946. Introduction by Edmund Blunden (see also entry 11). Consists of English Village (11); English Country Houses (15); British Ports And Harbours (35); English Cities And Small Towns (48); English Gardens (59); and English Inns (67). The text of each volume is complete and so are the colour illustrations except for Villages, which has lost four; but only Gardens has retained all its bw illustrations, the rest losing at least one and sometimes more.

136 Nature in Britain. W.J. Turner (Editor)
OV 324 pp, 48 cp, 132 bw. Pub 1946. No review in O or TLS. Introduction by Geoffrey Grigson (see also entry 65). Consists of The Birds Of Britain (36); Wild Life Of Britain (52); Wild Flowers Of Britain (65); British Marine Life (70); Trees In Britain (91); and Insect Life In Britain (94). Includes the full text of each of the volumes and all the colour plates except for four in Birds and four in Wild Life. Of the bw illustrations, five are missing from Birds, one from Wild Life, two from Marine Life, one from Trees and two from Insects.

137 British Adventure. W.J. Turner (Editor)
OV, 324 pp, 48 cp, 120 bw. Pub 1947, but probably shortly before the OV on Art listed next which records on the advertisement page this OV on Adventure. No review in O or TLS. Introduction by Nigel Tangye (see also entry 68). Consists of British Mountaineers (22); British Merchant Adventurers (27); British Soldiers (50); British Polar Explorers (53); British Seamen (58); and Britain In The Air (68). As with other OV, the texts are complete, but some illustrations have been omitted.

The Books

138 Aspects of British Art. W.J. Turner (Editor)
OV, 324 pp, 48 cp, 123 bw. Pub 1947. No review in O or TLS. Introduction by Michael Ayrton (see also entry 105). Consists of British Cartoonists (25); British Romantic Artists (34); British Portrait Painters (76); Sporting Pictures Of England (87); English Water Colour Painters (88); and British Drawings (105). As with other OV, the texts are complete, but some illustrations have been omitted.

139 British Craftsmanship. W.J. Turner (Editor)
OV, 322 pp, 48 cp, 152 bw. Pub 1948. No review in O or TLS. Introduction by W.B. Honey (see also entry 99). Consists of British Craftsmen (38); English Pottery And Porcelain (77); British Furniture Makers (89); English Glass (99); English Popular And Traditional Art (102); and British Clocks And Clockmakers (111). The texts of the individual volumes are reproduced complete as are all the colour plates. Most of the bw illustrations are also reproduced with between one and three illustrations omitted from each volume.

TITLES ANNOUNCED FOR FUTURE PUBLICATION BUT NOT PUBLISHED

Numbered titles included in chronological list above:

41 **Britain and The Middle East.** Sir Ronald Storrs

42 **Children's Verse.**

54 **English Conversation/British Conversationalists.** Lord David Cecil/Lettice Fowler

56 **British Biographies.** Rebecca West

114 **British Yachting.** C. St John Ellis

118 **British Humour.** D.B. Wyndham-Lewis

Un-numbered titles announced but not published:

British Textiles. Anne Scott-James

British Architecture. Robert Jordan

English Landscape. Geoffrey Grigson

Ireland. Prof. Walter Starkie

British Courage. Lord Moran

British/English Churches. John Betjeman

Matthew Arnold

Robert Browning

Cumulative Sales Figures to December 31, 1951, in Descending Order

The sales figures were prepared by Adprint's Company Secretary, Kenneth Helmore. A photo-copy of his original manuscript schedule was given to me by Joyce Howell who worked with him and who told Sheila Shannon that Kenneth Helmore had a reputation for precise work. His manuscript has been corrected by him in several places, which indicates his efforts to produce accurate figures. The full schedule contains figures for 119 volumes; there are no figures for the six volumes of the English Poets or for *Australia* (5) or for the omnibus volumes. The schedule prepared by Mr Helmore is arranged consecutively by volume number. Each entry starts with a column showing cumulative sales figures up to 1945 for each volume published before then; it goes on to show figures for each succeeding year, followed by a cumulative total up to the end of that year; and four final columns show figures for the year 1951, the cumulative figures to 31 December of that year, the figures for the total edition, and the books left unsold at end December 1951. From these figures I have prepared the summary schedule below, arranged in descending order of sales and showing the sales to end 1951, the total edition and the number still unsold at end 1951. I have added a column showing sales for 1952; this is based on information in a letter from William Collins to Kenneth Helmore dated 27 May 1953 which gives figures for the year 1 January to 31 December 1952. Some of these 1952 figures seem extraordinarily high; for example, 14,859 for *Wild Flowers in Britain* (65) and 11,239 for *Sporting Pictures of England* (87). I have concluded that these 1952 figures are for remaindered sales because of a letter from Adprint to authors of 22 December 1952 which recorded that Collins '... have been compelled to start remaindering the existing stock at a price considerably below cost.' The sales figures I quote in Part 1 are for sales up to end 1951, thus excluding the remaindered sales. There are some oddities about Mr Helmore's figures; for example sales sometimes exceed the edition figure and are described as oversold; and sometimes remaindered sales in 1952 exceed the stocks left unsold at end 1951. I understand that these discrepancies are not necessarily mistakes, but could arise from the way in which pages are printed and subsequently collated into complete volumes. I have commented on some of these discrepancies in the entries. Obviously the figures are not entirely accurate as there are sometimes mistakes of addition. However, the figures are valuable and certainly show the order of relative sales, making clear which were the most popular volumes. The figures correspond with the number of new impressions; and they are also compatible with figures given by Collins in a letter to Adprint of 29 July 1952 which lists deliveries of some of the volumes. I have recorded the figures exactly as they are written in the schedules or letters that I have seen and I have made no attempt to correct even obvious errors of addition. With all these reservations a summary of the figures follows.

The Books

TITLE	VOL NO.	SALES TO 31.12.51	TOTAL EDN.	UNSOLD 31.12.51	SALES 1952
The Birds of Britain	36	84,218	95,534	11,316	5,898
Life Among the English	31	61,636	50,540	Oversold	861
Wild Flowers in Britain	65	60,574	63,273	2,699	14,859
The English Poets	1	60,247	66,371	6,024	—
English Villages	11	56,883	62,440	5,557	104
Wild Life of Britain	52	56,822	79,024	22,262	8,805
The English Ballet	80	55,975	58,150	3,075	—
English Music	3	52,893	61,036	8,143	1,223
English Country Houses	15	51,606	46,158	Oversold	5,320
The Story of Scotland	21	51,105	57,647	6,542	139
English Inns	67	48,252	50,129	1,877	1,168
British Horses & Ponies	57	47,945	56,567	8,622	4,520
English Novelists	23	46,691	40,403	Oversold	5,572
British Postage Stamps	72	41,505	41,460	Oversold	—
English Gardens	59	41,176	44,481	3,305	2,912
Boy Scouts	75	40,598	40,181	Oversold	—
English Cricket	93	40,427	63,684	23,257	10,511
English Farming	16	39,848	41,108	1,260	89
English Pottery & China	77	39,512	40,082	570	—
English Cits & Sm Towns	48	38,108	45,417	7,709	1,958
The Story of Wales	62	36,196	39,595	3,399	2,443
British Dogs	96	34,694	45,962	11,268	8,594
British Maps & Map Mkrs	73	33,291	36,276	2,985	3,168
The English Bible	66	31,986	36,201	4,215	4,701
English Diaries & Jrnls	55	31,256	39,999	8,743	8,146
British Romantic Artists	34	30,146	32,857	2,711	2,102
British Craftsmen	38	29,315	29,385	70	—
British Furniture Makers	89	29,078	29,599	481	257
British Ports & H'bours	35	28,473	32,058	3,585	2,475
The Londoner	64	28,028	29,220	1,192	—
British Seamen	58	27,858	28,585	727	165
British Mountaineers	22	27,589	34,173	6,584	6,467
Sporting Pictures of Eng	87	27,422	41,055	13,633	11,239
Early Britain	92	27,115	33,074	5,959	1,617
English Public Schools	90	26,582	33,218	6,636	5,935
British Polar Explorers	53	26,265	32,850	6,585	6,042
British Clubs	63	26,254	36,341	10,087	7,197
Islands Round Britain	85	26,048	29,492	3,444	3,034
The Story of Ireland	39	25,986	29,188	3,202	—
The English at Table	51	25,769	25,635	Oversold	—
The Government of Britain	4	25,682	26,393	711	—
Canada	9	24,162	13,601	Oversold	—
British Garden Flowers	103	23,240	32,756	9,516	5,714
English Letter Writers	81	22,358	30,217	7,859	7,690

TITLE	VOL NO.	SALES TO 31.12.51	TOTAL EDN.	UNSOLD 31.12.51	SALES 1952
Life Among the Scots	101	21,316	26,220	4,904	5,387
Insect Life in Britain	94	21,095	34,571	13,481	7,425
English Glass	99	21,062	26,230	5,168	—
English Printed Books	95	20,867	30,180	9,313	8,888
British Botanists	79	20,730	29,207	8,477	8,487
The British Red Cross	74	20,398	19,740	Oversold	—
British Railways	83	20,292	25,284	4,992	5,072
British Statesmen	13	20,223	22,422	2,199	—
British Cartoonists C&CA	25	19,655	19,384	Oversold	—
English Children	30	19,329	19,571	242	—
English Women	29	19,025	19,458	433	—
English Education	17	18,898	17,079	Oversold	—
British Photographers	71	18,798	18,827	29	—
English Pop & Trad Art	102	18,612	26,977	8,365	5,009
English Rivers & Canals	84	18,462	25,273	6,811	7,512
British Soldiers	50	18,393	18,448	55	—
The English People	100	18,275	23,118	4,843	316
British Mchnt Advents	27	18,269	18,554	285	—
The Guilds of the C of L	82	18,232	25,438	7,206	6,803
British Rebels & Ref's	33	18,171	18,578	407	—
The British Colonial Emp	40	17,915	18,334	319	—
British Engineers	47	17,838	15,046	Oversold	—
English W'col Painters	88	17,825	18,043	825	—
Women's Institutes	61	17,486	17,927	441	—
British Golf	107	17,174	23,098	5,924	7,964
British Ships & Sh'drs	104	17,167	21,302	4,135	4,097
New Zealand	26	17,087	18,464	1,377	—
The English Church	28	16,859	17,267	408	—
British Marine Life	70	16,411	15,939	Oversold	—
Fairs Circuses & M'Halls	46	16,114	16,536	422	—
British Drawings	105	16,013	22,074	6,061	5,958
English Essayists	106	15,935	23,108	7,173	7,087
British Philosophers	60	15,756	15,725	Oversold	—
South Africa	18	15,736	16,770	1,034	—
British Scientists	14	15,711	17,702	1,991	153
Battlefields in Britain	78	15,556	15,755	199	—
The House of Commons	117	15,294	17,617	2,323	1,265
British Journalists & Ns	86	15,190	15,227	37	—
British Sea Fishermen	69	15,116	14,536	Oversold	—
Britain in the Air	68	15,018	14,420	Oversold	—
British Clocks & C'Mkrs	111	14,985	17,979	2,994	1,920
British Portrait Painters	76	14,547	14,654	107	—
British Weather	97	14,517	14,488	Oversold	—

The Books

TITLE	VOL NO.	SALES TO 31.12.51	TOTAL EDN.	UNSOLD 31.12.51	SALES 1952
Trees in Britain	91	14,306	14,407	101	—
British Dramatists	32	14,177	14,526	349	—
English Fashion	121	14,049	16,096	2,047	196
Roman Britain	113	14,022	21,677	7,655	4,202
British Sport	2	13,998	16,460	2,462	—
British Medicine	12	13,961	16,175	2,214	—
British Herbs & Veg	108	13,816	18,356	4,540	5,047
India	10	13,770	14,398	628	2
English Social Services	24	13,567	13,771	204	—
East Africa	6	13,474	14,273	899	—
British Universities	110	13,284	22,819	9,565	8,395
The British Theatre	119	13,203	15,664	2,861	—
English Hymns & H W'trs	98	11,758	17,892	6,034	5,143
The English at the S'ide	112	11,312	22,999	11,312	5,698
Brit Anglers' Nat Hist	109	10,802	18,300	7,498	2,754
British Orientalists	37	10,689	10,865	176	—
British Historians	49	10,611	10,883	272	—
English Cotts & Fmhses	128	10,586	15,095	4,509	4,095
British Trade Unions	45	9,598	9,536	Oversold	—
British Boxing	130	9,508	16,354	6,846	7,295
British W'mills & Wa'mills	120	9,415	15,888	6,473	4,468
The Turf	129	9,307	15,060	5,753	5,624
Children's Illus Books	126	9,302	14,910	5,608	1,920
British Chess	127	8,726	16,264	7,538	7,467
The Port of London	115	8,683	17,052	8,369	5,921
British Hills and Mts	116	8,226	15,172	6,946	3,096
The Conservative Party	122	7,870	12,060	4,190	3,443
British Hospitals	131	7,200	16,354	6,846	3,587
The Liberal Party	123	7,113	16,256	9,143	3,910
The Labour Party	124	6,961	12,383	5,422	3,207
British Butterflies	125	6,502	12,010	5,508	4,421
British Farm Stock	132	2,048	5,780	3,732	3,587

List of Authors and Editors

Authors and editors are styled as on title page of their volume. Reference numbers are to entries in the chronological list.

ADAM SMITH, Janet
Life Among the Scots, 101
Children's Illustrated Books, 126

ANSON, Peter F.
British Sea Fishermen, 69

ARBERRY, A.J.
British Orientalists, 37

AYRTON, Michael
British Drawings, 105

BARKER, Sir Ernest
British Statesmen, 13

BATCHELOR, Denzil
British Boxing, 130

BEATON, Cecil
British Photographers, 71

BELL, G.K.A. THE BISHOP OF CHICHESTER, G.K.A.
The English Church, 28

BETJEMAN, John
English Cities and Small Towns, 48

BICKNELL, Peter
British Hills and Mountains, 116

BIRCH, Nigel
The Conservative Party, 122

BLAKE, George
British Ships and Shipbuilders, 104

BLUNDEN, Edmund
English Villages, 11

BONE, Stephen
British Weather, 97

BOULENGER, E.G.
British Anglers' Natural History, 109

BOWEN, Elizabeth
English Novelists, 23

BURDEN (BURDON), R.M.
New Zealand, 26
Jointly with Ngaio Marsh

BURKE, Thomas
English Inns, 67

CARDUS, Neville
English Cricket, 93

CECIL, Lord David
The English Poets, 1

CHAPPELL, Metius
British Engineers, 47

CITRINE, Sir Walter
British Trade Unions, 45

COLLIS, Maurice
British Merchant Adventurers, 27

CRUIKSHANK, R.J.
The Liberal Party, 123

DARLING, F. Fraser
see FRASER DARLING

DARWIN, Bernard
British Clubs, 63
British Golf, 107

DAVIES, Rhys
The Story of Wales, 62

DISHER, M. Willson
Fairs, Circuses and Music Halls, 46

DOBRÉE, Bonamy
English Essayists, 106

ELTON, Arthur
British Railways, 83

The Books

EVANS, Admiral Sir Edward
British Polar Explorers, 53

EYRE, Frank
English Rivers and Canals, 84
Jointly with Charles Hadfield

FISHER, James
The Birds of Britain, 36

FOX, Adam
English Hymns and Hymn Writers, 98

FRASER DARLING, F.
The Story of Scotland, 21
Wild Life of Britain, 52

GILMOUR, John
British Botanists, 79

GLOAG, John
British Furniture Makers, 89

GREENE, Graham
British Dramatists, 32

GREGORY, Sir Richard
British Scientists, 14

GRIERSON, Sir Herbert
The English Bible, 66

GRIGSON, Geoffrey
Wild Flowers in Britain, 65

HADFIELD, Charles
English Rivers and Canals, 84
Jointly with Frank Eyre

HALL, William Glenvil
The Labour Party, 124

HAMPSON, John
The English at Table, 51

HASKELL, Arnold
Australia, 5

HAWKES, Jacquetta
Early Britain, 92

HENNELL, T.
British Craftsmen, 38

HERBERT, John
The Port of London, 115

HISLOP, John
The Turf, 129

HONEY, W. B.
English Glass, 99

HOWARD, Alexander L.
Trees in Britain, 91

HUDSON, Derek
British Journalists and Newspapers, 86

HUXLEY, Elspeth
East Africa, 6

IVES, A. G. L.
British Hospitals, 131

JOHNSON, S. C.
British Postage Stamps, 72

JOHNSTON, S. H. F.
British Soldiers, 50

LAMBERT, Margaret
English Popular and Traditional Art, 102
Jointly with Enid Marx

LINDSAY, Kenneth
English Education, 17

LINDSAY MP, Martin
The House of Commons, 117

LOCKLEY, R. M.
Islands Round Britain, 85

LOW, David
British Cartoonists, Caricaturists and Comic Artists, 25

LYNAM, Edward
British Maps and Mapmakers, 73

LYND, Sylvia
English Children, 30

MACAULAY, Rose
Life Among the English, 31

McCALL, Cicely
Women's Institutes, 61

McNAIR WILSON, R.
see WILSON

MARSDEN, Christopher
The English at the Seaside, 112

MARSH, Ngaio
New Zealand, 26
Jointly with R. Burden (Burdon)

MARX, Enid
English Popular and Traditional Art, 24
Jointly with Margaret Lambert

MATHEW, David
British Seamen, 58

MATTHEWS, Kenneth
British Philosophers, 60
British Chess, 127

MEYNELL, Francis
English Printed Books, 95

MILES, Bernard
The British Theatre, 119

MILLIN, Sarah Gertrude
South Africa, 18

MORRAH, Dermot
The British Red Cross, 74

NEWMAN, Sir George
English Social Services, 24

NICHOLSON, Lady
The Londoner, 64

NOON, Sir Firozkhan
India, 10

O'BRIEN, Kate
English Diaries and Journals, 55

O'FAOLAIN, Sean
The Story of Ireland, 39

ORWELL, George
The English People, 100

PAGET, Guy
Sporting Pictures of England, 87

PARIS, H.J.
English Watercolour Painters, 88

PARKER, Eric
British Sport, 2

PIPER, John
British Romantic Artists, 34

POOLEY, Sir Ernest
The Guilds of the City of London, 82

PORTSMOUTH, The Earl of
British Farm Stock, 132

REYNOLDS, E.E.
Boy Scouts, 75

RICHMOND, Ian
Roman Britain, 113

ROBERTS, Harry
British Rebels and Reformers, 33
English Gardens, 59

ROBERTS, S.C.
British Universities, 110

RUSSELL, Sir John
English Farming, 16

RUSSELL, John
British Portrait Painters, 76

SABINE, Noel
The British Colonial Empire, 40

SACKVILLE-WEST, V.
English Country Houses, 15

SEMPILL, Cecilia
English Pottery and China, 77

SETTLE, Alison
English Fashion, 121

SITWELL, Edith
English Women, 29

SKILTON, C.P.
British Windmills and Watermills, 120

SMITH, A. Croxton
British Dogs, 96

SMITH, Janet Adam
see ADAM SMITH

SMYTHE, F.S.
British Mountaineers, 22

TANGYE, Nigel
Britain in the Air, 68

The Books

TAYLOR, Geoffrey
Insect Life in Britain, 94

TAYLOR, George M.
British Garden Flowers, 103
British Herbs and Vegetables, 108

TEMPLE, Vere
British Butterflies, 124

TURNER, W.J.
English Music, 3
The English Ballet, 80
The British Commonwealth and Empire OV, 131
Impressions of English Literature OV, 134
The Englishman's Country OV, 135
Nature in Britain OV, 136
British Adventure OV, 137
Aspects of British Art OV, 138
British Craftsmanship OV, 139
The seven OV all edited by W.J. Turner

TWEEDSMUIR, Lady
Canada, 9

ULLYETT, Kenneth
British Clocks and Clockmakers, 111

VULLIAMY, C.E.
English Letter Writers, 81

WALMSLEY, Leo
British Ports and Harbours, 35

WARNER, Rex
English Public Schools, 90

WARREN, C. Henry
English Cottages and Farmhouses, 128

WEDGWOOD, C.V.
Battlefields in Britain, 78

WELLESLEY, Dorothy
Shelley, 7
Byron, 8
Tennyson, 19
Keats, 20
Coleridge, 43
Wordsworth, 44
The six volumes of English Poets all edited by Dorothy Wellesley.

WENTWORTH, Lady
British Horses and Ponies, 57

WILSON, R. McNair
British Medicine, 12

WOODWARD, E.L.
British Historians, 49

YONGE, C.M.
British Marine Life, 70

YOUNG, G.M.
The Government of Britain, 4

Subject List

This list arranges BIP books into the three series of 'The British People In Pictures', 'The British Commonwealth In Pictures' and 'The English Poets In Pictures'. The People books are further arranged according to the nine subject groups within which they were usually advertised on the lower dust-jacket. The seven omnibus volumes, sometimes advertised as Guinea Books, are also shown. (For the benefit of younger readers I should perhaps explain that a guinea in Britain's pre-decimal coinage was one pound and one shilling, in figures shown thus: £1.1s. The decimal equivalent now is £1.05.) Numbers refer to entries in the chronological list.

A THE BRITISH PEOPLE IN PICTURES

A1 History and Achievement

The Government of Britain, G.M. Young, 4
British Statesmen, Sir Ernest Barker, 13
British Mountaineers, F.S. Smythe, 22
British Merchant Adventurers, Maurice Collis, 27
British Soldiers, S.H.F. Johnston, 50
British Polar Explorers, Admiral Sir Edward Evans, 53
British Seamen, David Mathew, 58
Britain in the Air, Nigel Tangye, 68
British Sea Fishermen, Peter F. Anson, 69
Battlefields in Britain, C.V. Wedgwood, 78
The Guilds of the City of London, Sir Ernest Pooley, 82
Early Britain, Jacquetta Hawkes, 92
Roman Britain, Ian Richmond, 113
The House of Commons, Martin Lindsay MP, 117
The Conservative Party, Nigel Birch, 122
The Liberal Party, R.J. Cruikshank, 123
The Labour Party, William Glenvil Hall, 124
British Courage, not numbered or published

A2 Art and Craftsmanship

English Music, W.J. Turner, 3
British Cartoonists, Caricaturists and Comic Artists, David Low, 25
British Romantic Artists, John Piper, 34
British Craftsmen, T. Hennell, 38
British Photographers, Cecil Beaton, 71
British Postage Stamps, S.C. Johnson, 72
British Portrait Painters, John Russell, 76
English Pottery and China, Cecilia Sempill, 77
The English Ballet, W.J. Turner, 80

Sporting Pictures of England, Guy Paget, 87
English Watercolour Painters, H.J. Paris, 88
British Furniture Makers, John Gloag, 89
English Printed Books, Francis Meynell, 95
English Glass, W.B. Honey, 99
English Popular and Traditional Art, Enid Marx and Margaret Lambert, 102
British Drawings, Michael Ayrton, 105
British Clocks and Clockmakers, Kenneth Ullyett, 111
The British Theatre, Bernard Miles, 119
Children's Illustrated Books, Janet Adam Smith, 126
British Architecture, Robert Jordan, not numbered or published
British Textiles, Anne Scott-James, not numbered or published

A3 Literature and Belles Lettres

The English Poets, Lord David Cecil, 1
English Novelists, Elizabeth Bowen, 23
British Dramatists, Graham Greene, 32
British Orientalists, A.J. Arberry, 37
British Historians, E.L. Woodward, 49
English Diaries and Journals, Kate O'Brien, 55
British Biographies, Rebecca West, 56 not published
British Philosophers, Kenneth Matthews, 60
English Letter Writers, C.E. Vulliamy, 81
British Journalists and Newspapers, Derek Hudson, 86
English Essayists, Bonamy Dobrée, 106

A4 Education and Religion

English Education, Kenneth Lindsay, 17
The English Church, The Bishop of Chichester G.K.A. Bell, 28
The English Bible, Sir Herbert Grierson, 66
English Public Schools, Rex Warner, 90
English Hymns and Hymn Writers, Adam Fox, 98
British Universities, S.C. Roberts, 110
British Churches, not numbered or published

A5 Science, Medicine and Engineering

British Medicine, R. McNair Wilson, 12
British Scientists, Sir Richard Gregory, 14
English Social Services, Sir George Newman, 24
British Engineers, Metius Chappell, 47
British Maps and Mapmakers, Edward Lynam, 73
The British Red Cross, Dermot Morrah, 74
British Railways, Arthur Elton, 83
British Weather, Stephen Bone, 97
British Ships and Shipbuilders, George Blake, 104

British Windmills and Watermills, C.P. Skilton, 120
British Hospitals, A.G.L. Ives, 131

A6   Social Life and Character

English Women, Edith Sitwell, 29
English Children, Sylvia Lynd, 30
Life Among the English, Rose Macaulay, 31
British Rebels and Reformers, Harry Roberts, 33
British Trade Unions, Sir Walter Citrine, 45
Fairs, Circuses and Music Halls, M. Willson Disher, 46
The English at Table, John Hampson, 51
English Conversation, Lettice Fowler, 54 not published
Women's Institutes, Cicely McCall, 61
British Clubs, Bernard Darwin, 63
The Londoner, Lady Nicholson, 64
Boy Scouts, E.E. Reynolds, 75
The English People, George Orwell, 100
Life Among the Scots, Janet Adam Smith, 101
The English at the Seaside, Christopher Marsden, 112
British Humour, D.B. Wyndham-Lewis, 118 not published
English Fashion, Alison Settle, 121
British Chess, Kenneth Mathews, 127

A7   Topographical History

The Story of Scotland, F. Fraser Darling, 21
British Ports and Harbours, Leo Walmsley, 35
The Story of Ireland, Sean O'Faolain, 39
English Cities and Small Towns, John Betjeman, 48
The Story of Wales, Rhys Davies, 62
English Rivers and Canals, Frank Eyre and Charles Hadfield, 84
Islands Round Britain, R.M. Lockley, 85
The Port of London, John Herbert, 115
British Hills and Mountains, Peter Bicknell, 116
English Landscape, Geoffrey Grigson, not numbered or published

A8   Country Life and Sport

British Sport, Eric Parker, 2
English Villages, Edmund Blunden, 11
English Country Houses, V. Sackville-West, 15
English Farming, Sir John Russell, 16
British Horses and Ponies, Lady Wentworth, 57
English Gardens, Harry Roberts, 59
English Inns, Thomas Burke, 67
English Cricket, Neville Cardus, 93
British Dogs, A. Croxton Smith, 96

British Garden Flowers, George M. Taylor, 103
British Golf, Bernard Darwin, 107
British Herbs and Vegetables, George M. Taylor, 108
British Yachting, C. St. John Ellis, 114, not published
English Cottages and Farmhouses, C. Henry Warren, 128
The Turf, John Hislop, 129
British Boxing, Denzil Batchelor, 130
British Farm Stock, The Earl of Portsmouth, 132

A9   Natural History

The Birds of Britain, James Fisher, 36
Wild Life of Britain, F. Fraser Darling, 52
Wild Flowers in Britain, Geoffrey Grigson, 65
British Marine Life, C.M. Yonge, 70
British Botanists, John Gilmour, 79
Trees in Britain, Alexander L. Howard, 91
Insect Life in Britain, Geoffrey Taylor, 94
British Anglers' Natural History, E.G. Boulenger, 109
British Butterflies, Vere Temple, 125

B   THE BRITISH COMMONWEALTH IN PICTURES

Australia, Arnold Haskell, 5
East Africa, Elspeth Huxley, 6
Canada, Lady Tweedsmuir, 9
India, Sir Firozkhan Noon, 10
South Africa, Sarah Gertrude Millin, 18
New Zealand, Ngaio Marsh and R. Burden (Burdon), 26
The British Colonial Empire, Noel Sabine, 40

C   THE ENGLISH POETS IN PICTURES

Shelley, 7
Byron, 8
Tennyson, 19
Keats, 20
Coleridge, 43
Wordsworth, 44

All edited by Dorothy Wellesley

D OMNIBUS VOLUMES

The British Commonwealth and Empire, 133
Impressions of English Literature, 134
The Englishman's Country, 135
Nature in Britain, 136
British Adventure, 137
Aspects of British Art, 138
British Craftsmanship, 139

All edited by W.J. Turner.

INDEX

Numbers in brackets refer to the volume number in the chronological list in Part 2. Other numbers refer to pages in both parts. Volume titles start with a substantive word, followed when appropriate by the definite article. When cross references would be helpful, the cross reference title has been split or shortened; thus *East Africa* can be found also as *Africa, East*, and *Fairs, Circuses and Music Halls* can be found also under *Circuses* and *Music Halls*. Book titles whether full, split or shortened, are always in italics.

Aberystwyth, paintings stored in, 46
Adam Smith, Janet, (101), (126), 9, 48
Adprint, 8, 14, 17, 21, 23-27, 29, 37, 41, 46, 67-68
Adventure, (137)
Africa, East, (6), 9, 30, 42, 52
Africa, South, (18), 42, 48, 55
Air, Britain in the, (68)
Aldus Books, 26
Anglers' Natural History, (109)
Anson, Peter F., (69)
Antiquarian Book Monthly, 8, 14
Arberry, A.J., (37)
Architecture, 119
Art, Popular and Traditional, (102), 9, 37, 48, 49
Artists, British Romantic, (34), 48, 52
Aspects of British Art, (138)
Astor, Lady, 18, 33
Australia, (5), 30, 51, 52, 74
Ayrton, Michael, (105), 59

Bahamas editions, 29, 73
Ballet, (80), 36, 44
Barker, Sir Ernest, (13), 51, 52
Bartlett, Vernon, 18
Batchelor, Denzil, (130), 50
Battlefields in Britain, (78), 9, 15, 45, 52
BBC, 17, 21
Beaton, Cecil, (71), 46
Bell, Bishop G.K.A., (28), 53
Betjeman, John, (48), 36, 44, 50
Bible, The English, (66), 42
Bicknell, Peter, (116), 9, 33, 46, 48
Birch, Nigel, (122)
Biographies, (56)
Birds of Britain, (36), 36, 44, 48
Blake, George, (104), 58
Blitz, The, 13, 30, 31, 35, 43-45
Blunden, Edmund, (11), 37, 44, 45, 50, 57, 59
Bone, Stephen, (97)
Books: *Children's Illustrated*, (126), 9, 48, 67
 English Printed, (95)

Books:
 Sub-committee on supply of, 7, 35
Botanists, (79), 53
Boulenger, E.G., (109)
Bowen, Elizabeth, (23), 36, 50
Boxing, (130)
Boy Scouts, (75)
Bracken Books, 73
Breman, Paul, 8, 65, 73
Briggs, Asa, see BBC
Britain in the Air, (68)
— *Battlefields in*, (78), 9, 15, 45, 52
— *Birds of*, (36), 36, 44, 48
— *Early*, (92)
— *Government of*, (4), 49
— *Insect Life in*, (94)
— *Islands Round* (85)
— *and the Middle East*, (41)
— *Roman*, (113), 36, 58, 74
— *Trees in*, (91)
— *Wild Flowers in*, (65), 36, 47
— *Wild Life of*, (52), 36
British Anglers' Natural History, (109)
— *Biographies*, (56)
— *Botanists*, (79), 53
— *Boxing*, (130)
— *Butterflies*, (125), 38, 46, 67
— *Cartoonists, Caricaturists and Comic Artists*, (25), 44, 53
— *Chess*, (127)
— *Clocks and Clockmakers*, (111), 74
— *Clubs*, (63)
— *Colonial Empire, The*, (40)
— *Commonwealth in Pictures, The*, (5), (6), (9), (10), (18), (26), (40), (133), 14, 42, 66, 71
— *Conversationalists*, (54)
— *Craftsmen*, (38), 52, 59
— *Dogs*, (96), 38
— *Dramatists*, (32), 50
— *Drawings*, (105), 59
— *Engineers*, (47), 53
— *Farm Stock*, (132), 58, 65, 67
— *Furniture Makers*, (89), 59
— *Garden Flowers*, (103)

British
— *Golf*, (107)
— *Herbs and Vegetables*, (108)
— *Hills and Mountains*, (116), 9, 33, 46, 48
— *Historians*, (49), 47
— *Horses and Ponies*, (57), 36, 38, 51
— *Hospitals*, (131), 8, 44
— *Humour*, (118)
— *Journalists and Newspapers*, (86), 9, 33
— *Maps and Map Makers*, (73)
— *Marine Life*, (70)
— *Medicine*, (12), 44, 53
— *Merchant Adventurers*, (27)
— *Mountaineers*, (22), 48, 54
— *Orientalists*, (37)
— *People in Pictures*, 14, 41, 66, 71
— *Philosophers*, (60), 55-57
— *Photographers*, (71), 44, 46, 73
— *Polar Explorers*, (53), 53-54
— *Portrait Painters*, (76)
— *Ports and Harbours*, (35), 53, 55
— *Postage Stamps*, (72), 37, 48
— *Railways*, (83)
— *Rebels and Reformers*, (33)
— *Red Cross, The*, (74)
— *Romantic Artists*, (34), 48, 52
— *Scientists*, (14), 52
— *Sea Fishermen*, (69)
— *Seamen*, (58)
— *Ships and Shipbuilders*, (104), 58
— *Soldiers*, (50), 51, 72
— *Sport*, (2), 30
— *Statesmen*, (13), 51, 52
— *Theatre*, (119)
— *Trade Unions*, (45), 51
— *Universities*, (110)
— *Weather*, (97)
— *Windmills and Watermills*, (120)
— *Yachting*, (114)
Butterflies, (125), 38, 46, 67
Burdon (Burden), R.M., (26), 8, 30, 34, 49, 50, 71
Burke, Thomas, (67)

Index

Burne-Jones, Sir Edward, 51
Byron, (8), 30, 51

Canada, (9)
Canals, Rivers and, (84), 9, 16, 35, 57, 72
Cardus, Neville, (93), 42, 48, 50
Caricaturists, (25), 44, 53
Cartoonists, (25), 44, 53
Cecil, Lord David, (1), 15, 17, 36, 61, 69
Chappell, Metius, (47), 53
Chatham House, 20
Chess, British, (127)
Children, English, (38), 44
Children's Illustrated Books, (126), 9, 48, 67
China, Pottery and, (77), 59, 65, 73
Church, The English, (28), 53
Churches, British/English, 119
Circuses, (46), 53
Cities and Small Towns, (48), 36
Citrine, (Lord), (45), 51
Clocks and Clockmakers, (111), 74
Clubs, British, (63)
Coleridge, (43)
Colonial Empire, The British, (40)
Collins, Sir William, 24, 34
Collins, William, (publisher), 7, 17, 23, 26, 27, 31, 33, 34, 36-38, 67, 68, 73
Collis, Maurice, (27)
Comic Artists, (25), 44, 53
Commonwealth, see British
Commons, The House of, (117), 52
Conservative Party, The, (122)
Contracts — publishing, 26, 27
Conversationalists, (54)
Cottages and Farmhouses, (128)
Country Houses, (15), 36, 42
Courage, (119)
Craftmanship, (139)
Craftsmen, (38), 52, 59
Cricket, (93), 36, 42, 48
Cruikshank, R.J., (123)

Daily Herald, 23
Daily Telegraph, The, 60
Dalby, Richard, 8
Darling, see Fraser Darling
Darwin, Bernard, (63), (107), 50
Davies, Rhys, (62), 50
De Beer, Professor E.S., 47
Diaries and Journals, (55), 51, 53
Dickinson, Mrs Patric — see Shannon
Dictionary of National Biography, 39, 74
Disher, M. Willson, (46), 53
Dobrée, Bonamy, (106)
Dogs, British, (96), 38
Dramatists, (32), 50

Drawings, (105), 59

Eads, Peter, 8, 17, 27, 65, 68
Early Britain, (92), 9, 16, 36, 52, 74
East Africa, (6), 9, 42, 52
Education, (17)
Elton, Arthur, (83)
Empire, see British
Engineers, (47), 53
English Ballet, The, (80), 36, 44
— Bible, The, (66), 42
— Children, (30), 44
— Church, The, (28), 53
— Cities and Small Towns, (48), 36, 44
— Conversation, (54)
— Cottages and Farmhouses, (128)
— Country Houses, (15), 36, 42
— Cricket, (93), 36, 42, 45
— Diaries and Journals, (55), 51, 53
— Education, (17)
— Essayists, (106)
— Farming, (16), 8
— Fashion, (121), 36
— Gardens, (59), 36
— Glass, (99), 36
— Inns, (67), 37
— Hymns and Hymn Writers, (98), 42
— Letter Writers, (81), 70
— Life Among the, (31), 36, 42, 44, 53
— Music, (3), 30, 37, 46
— Novelists, (23), 36
— People, The, (100), 36, 42, 44, 47, 65
— Poets, (1), 15, 30, 36
— Poets in Pictures, The, (7), (8), (19), (20), (43), (44), 14, 32, 42, 66, 71
— Popular and Traditional Art, (102), 9, 37, 48, 59
— Pottery and China, (77), 33, 59, 65, 73
— Printed Books, (95)
— Public Schools, (90), 47
— Rivers and Canals, (84), 9, 16, 35, 57, 72
— at the Seaside, (112), 8, 58
— Social Services, (24)
— at Table, (51), 44, 72
— Villages, (11), 37, 44, 59
— Watercolour Painters, (88), 73
— Women, (29), 34, 37, 42, 53
Englishman's Country, The, (135), 45
Essayists, (106)
Evacuees, 43, 44
Evans, Admiral Sir Edward, (53), 53-54
Explorers, British Polar, (53), 53-54

Eyre, Frank, (84), 9, 16, 33, 35

Fables, Parables and Plots, 39
Fairs, Circuses and Music Halls, (46), 53
Farm Stock, (132), 58, 65, 67
Farming, (16)
Farmhouses, Cottages and, (128)
Fashion, (121), 36
Festival of Britain, 36, 41, 42
Fielden, Lionel, 20, 32
Fisher, H.A.L., Mrs and Mary, 23, 33
Fisher, James, (36), 33, 36, 44
Fishermen, Sea, (69)
Fleetwood-Walker, B., 44
Flowers, Garden, (103)
— Wild, (65), 36
Foges, Wolfgang, 9, 17, 24-29, 41, 49
Fox, Adam, (98)
Fraser Darling, F., (21), (52), 36, 59
Fraser, Sir Robert, 29
Friedlander, Elisabeth, 25
Furniture Makers, (89), 59

Gardens, (59), 36
Garden Flowers, (103)
Garland, Nicholas, 60
Garvin, J.L., 31
Gilmour, John, (79), 53
Glass, (99), 36
Gloag, John, (89), 59
Goebbels, see War
Goldsack, Sidney, 25
Golf, British, (107)
Government of Britain, The, (4), 49
Greene, Graham, (32), 50, 65
Gregory, Sir Richard, (14), 51
Grierson, Sir Herbert, (66)
Grigson, Geoffrey, (65), 36, 47, 59
Guilds Of The City Of London, (82)

Hadfield, Charles, (84), 9, 27, 33, 35, 72
Hailey, Lord, 20
Hall, William Glenvil, (124)
Hampson, John, (51)
Harbours, Ports and, (35), 53, 55
Harrap, Alice, 8, 26, 29
Haskell, Arnold, (5), 30, 51, 52
Hawkes, Jacquetta, (92), 9, 16, 36, 39, 52
Helmore, K., 37, 120
Helpman, Robert, 13
Hengelo, Sadler's Wells visit to, 13
Hennell, T., (38), 52, 59
Herbert, A.P., 31, 112

Index

Herbert, John, (115), 9
Herbs and Vegetables, (108)
Hicks, Joynson, 18
Hills and Mountains, (116), 9, 33, 46, 48
Hinde, John, 46
Hislop, John, (129), 9
Historians, (49), 47
Hitler, see War
Honey, W.B., (99), 36
Howard, Alexander L., (91)
Hobbs, Juliet, 8, 30
Horses and Ponies, (57), 63, 51
Hospitals, (131), 8, 44
House Of Commons, The, (117), 52
Howell, Joyce, 8, 26
Hudson, Derek, (86), 9, 33, 34, 50
Humour, British, (118)
Huxley, Elspeth, (6), 9, 42, 52
Hymns and Hymn Writers, (98), 42

Illustrated Books, Children's, (126), 48, 67
Illustrations, number and quality of, 45-49, 71
Impressions of English Literature, (134)
In the Air, (68)
India, (10)
Information, Ministry of, 13, 21, 28
Inns, (67), 37
Insect Life, (94)
Institutes, Women's, (61), 43
Ireland, The Story of, (39)
Islands Round Britain, (85), 9, 16,
Ives, A.G.L., (131), 8

Joint Broadcasting Committee (JBC), 21, 22, 23, 27, 28
Johnson, S.C., (72)
Johnston, S.H.F., (50), 51
Journalists, (86), 9, 33
Journals, Diaries and, (55), 51, 53

Keats, (20)
Kennedy, Ambassador Joseph, 13
King Penguins, 25, 49
Kinnane, John, 8

Labour Party, The, (124)
Lambert, Margaret, (102), 9, 37, 48, 59
Landscape, English, 119
Lane, Allen, 23, 25
Lawrence, T.E., 18
Letter Writers, (81), 70
Liberal Party, The, (123)
Life Among the English, (31), 36, 42, 44, 53
Life Among the Scots, (101), 9

Lindsay, Kenneth, (17)
Lindsay MP, Sir Martin, (117), 52
Listener, The, 8, 29, 33, 42, 46, 49, 57
Lockley, R.M. (85), 9, 16
Low, David, (25), 44, 53
Literature, Impressions of, (134)
London Mercury, The, 23
London, The Port Of, (115), 9
Londoner, The, (64), 44
Lynam, Edward, (73)
Lynd, Sylvia, (30), 44

Macaulay, Rose, (31), 42, 44, 50, 53, 57
McCall, Cicely, (61), 43
McNair, see Wilson
Maps and Mapmakers, (73)
Marine Life, (70)
Marsden, Christopher, (112), 8, 58
Marsh, Ngaio, (26), 8, 30, 34, 49, 50, 71
Martin, Kingsley, 39
Marx, Enid, (24), 9, 37, 48, 59
Matheson, Hilda, 8, 12, 14, 16-23, 27, 28, 31-33, 40, 69
Mathew, David, (58)
Matthews, Kenneth, (60), (127), 55-57
Medicine, British, (12), 44, 53
Merchant Adventurers, (27)
Meynell, Francis, (95)
Middle East, The, (41)
Miles, Bernard, (119)
Millin, Sarah, Gertrude, (18), 42, 55, 57
Mills, Brian, 8, 14
Ministry of Information, 13, 21, 28
Morrell, Lady Ottoline, 23
Morrah, Dermot, (74)
Mosley, (Sir) Oswald, 18
Mountaineers, (22), 48, 54
Mountains, Hills and, (116), 9, 33, 46, 48
Murdoch, J.S.M., 8, 73
Music, English, (3), 37, 46
Music Halls, (46), 53

Nassau, Adprint office in, 29, 73
Natural History, Anglers', (109)
Nature in Britain, (136)
Neurath, Eva, 8, 24, 26
— Walter, 8, 24, 25, 26, 28, 49
New Statesman and Nation, 8, 19, 23, 39, 57
New Zealand, (26), 49
News Chronicle, 8, 19, 20
Newman, Sir George, (24)
Newspapers, (86), 9, 33
Nicolson, Sir Harold, 18

Nicolson, Nigel, 8, 27
Nicholson, Lady, (64)
Novelists, (23), 36
Noon, (Sir) Firozkhan, (10)

O'Brien, Kate, (55), 50, 51, 53, 60
O'Faolain, Sean, (39)
Observer, The, 8, 30, 31, 34-35, 39, 48, 57, 70, 72
Omnibus volumes, (133)-(139), 74
Orientalists, British, (37)
Orwell, George, (100), 37, 42, 47, 50, 58, 65

Paget, Guy, (87), 58
Paris, H.J., (88)
Parish, Max, 29
Parker, Eric, (2)
Penguin Books, 23, 38
Penns in the Rocks, 17, 22, 26, 32, 67
People, (100), 36, 42, 44, 47, 65
Petter, Mary, 25, 26
Philosophers, (60), 55-57
Photographers, (71), 44, 46, 73
Picture Post, 46
Piper, John, (34), 48, 49, 52
Planning and Broadcasting Committee, 13
Poets, (1), 36
Polar Explorers, (53), 53-54
Ponies, Horses and, (57), 36, 51
Pooley, Sir Ernest, (82)
Popular and Traditional Art, (102), 9, 37, 48, 59
Port of London, The, (115), 9
Portrait Painters, (76)
Ports and Harbours, (35), 53, 55
Portsmouth, The Earl of, (132), 58
Postage Stamps, (72), 37, 48
Pottery and China, (77), 59, 65, 73
Price, Dr William, 50
Prices, of BIP books, 14, 26, 35, 38, 42
Priestley, Mrs J.B., see Hawkes
Princess Elizabeth, The, 41
Printed Books, (95)
Printers of BIP, 68
Private Library, The, 8, 65, 68, 73
Propaganda, 13, 14, 21, 28-30
Profitability, of BIP, 38
Public Schools, (90), 47
Publishers' Association, 35

Railways, British, (83)
Rayner, John, 48
Rebels and Reformers, (33)
Recording Britain, 58
Red Cross, The, (74)
Reith, (Lord), 18-20
Reviewers' opinions, 57
Reynolds, E.E., (75)

Index

Richmond, Ian, (133), 37, 58
Rivers and Canals, (84), 9, 16, 35, 57, 72
Roberts, Harry, (33), 36
Roberts, S.C., (110)
Roman Britain, (113), 36, 58, 74
Romantic Artists, (34), 48, 52
Rosenberg, Ruth, 8, 26, 27
Russell, John, (76)
Russell, Sir John, (16)

Sabine, Noel, (40)
Sackville-West, V., (15), 18, 22, 27, 31, 36, 38, 42, 57
Sadlers Wells Ballet, 13, 44
Sassoon, Siegfried, 23
Savile Club, 39
Sales, of BIP books, 35-38, 120-123
Schnabel, Artur, 41
Schools, Public, (90)
Scientists, (14), 51
Scotland, The Story of, (21), 37
Scots, Life Among, (101), 9
Scott-James, Anne, 9
Scouts, Boy, (75), 37
Sea Fishermen, (69)
Seamen, (58)
Seaside, (112), 58
Sedgeley, M., 8, 73
Sempill, Lady Cecilia, (77), 33, 59
Settle, Alison, (121), 37
Shelley, (7), 30, 42
Shannon, Sheila, 9, 17, 23-24, 25, 27-29, 32-35, 39, 40, 43, 46, 54
Ships and Shipbuilders, (104), 58
Sitwell, Edith, (29), 23, 34, 37, 42, 50, 53
Skilton, C.P., (120)
Small Towns, Cities and, (48), 36, 44
Smith, A. Croxton, (96)
Smith, F.T., 25
Smith, Janet, see Adam Smith

Smythe, F.S., (22), 54
Social Services, (24)
Soldiers, (50), 51, 72
South Africa, (18), 42, 48, 55
Spectator, The, 8, 23, 30, 57
Sport, (2)
Sporting Pictures of England, (87), 73
Stamps, Postage, (72), 37, 48
Statesmen, (13), 51, 52
Stationers' Hall, bombing of, 13, 31, 55
Stonier, G.W., 35
Storrs, Sir Ronald, 17, 29
Story of Ireland, The, (39)
Story of Scotland, The, (21), 37
Story of Wales, The, (62), 48, 50

Table, The English at, (51), 72
Tangye, Nigel, (68), 8
Taylor, Geoffrey, (94)
Taylor, George M., (103), (108)
Temple, Vere, (125), 38, 46
Tennyson, (19)
Textiles, 119
Thames and Hudson, 8, 26
Theatre, The, (119)
Times, The, 8, 20, 33, 52, 55, 57, 74
Times Literary Supplement, The, 8, 15, 38, 39, 52, 53, 55, 57, 59, 70, 72
Trade Unions, (45), 51
Translations, 14, 51
Trees in Britain, (91)
Turf, The, (129), 9
Turner, Delphine, 41
Turner, W.J., (3), (80), (131-9), 9, 16, 22-23, 26, 28, 31-35, 38, 39-41, 46, 50, 52, 54, 69, 72, 112
Tweedsmuir, Lady, (9)

Ullman, Elisabeth, 25, 26
Ullyett, Kenneth, (111)

Unions, Trade, (45), 57
Universities, (110)

Vegetables, Herbs and, (108)
Villages, (11), 37, 44, 59
Vulliamy, C.E., (81), 70

Wales, The Story of, (62), 48, 50
Walmsley, Leo, (35), 53, 55
Walpole, Sir Hugh, 17, 29
Walton, (Sir) William, 23
War: 1914-18, 17
— 1939-45, 13, 21, 25, 30-31, 34, 35, 43-45
Warner, Rex, (90), 47
Warren, C. Henry, (128)
Watercolour Painters, (88), 73
Weather, (97)
Wedgwood, C.V., (78), 9, 15, 16, 45, 52
Wellesley, Dorothy, (7), (8), (19), (20), (43), (44), 16, 18, 21-22, 32, 50, 67, 69, 72
Wentworth, Lady, (57), 36, 51
Whyte, Sir Frederick, 17, 28
Wickham, D.E., 8, 73
Wild Flowers in Britain, (65), 36, 47
Wild Life of Britain, (52), 36
Wilson, R. McNair, (12), 44, 53, 57
Windmills and Watermills, (120)
Winnant, Ambassador John, 31
Wood, Noel Mewton, 41
Woodward, E.L., (49), 47, 50
Woolf, Virginia, 18, 21, 32
Women, (29), 34, 37, 42, 53
Women's Institutes, (61), 43
Wordsworth, (44)

Yachting, (114)
Yeats: temple to, 22, 32, 67
— W.B., 22, 23, 39
Yonge, C.M., (70), 59
Young, G.M., (4), 15, 43, 48, 50